PRINTING IN LONDON

Loe here the forme and figure of the preſſe
Moſt liuelily obiected to thine eye.
The worth whereof no tongue can well expreſſe
So much it doth, and workes ſo readily:
For which let's giue vnto the Lord all praiſe,
That thus hath bleſſ'd vs in theſe latter daies.

1 Printing in London was performed in small offices
such as the above for more than three centuries. The
wooden hand press was about six feet high. (Block, $2\frac{5}{8}$
$\times$ 3 in.)

PRINTING IN LONDON

FROM 1476 TO MODERN TIMES

COMPETITIVE PRACTICE AND

TECHNICAL INVENTION

IN THE TRADE OF

BOOK AND BIBLE PRINTING

PERIODICAL PRODUCTION

JOBBING

&c

P. M. HANDOVER

M.A. F.R.HIST.S.

Ruskin House

GEORGE ALLEN & UNWIN LTD

MUSEUM STREET LONDON

FIRST PUBLISHED IN 1960

© P. M. Handover, 1960

PRINTED IN GREAT BRITAIN
in 11 on 12 pt. Ehrhardt
BY SIMSON SHAND LTD
LONDON, HERTFORD AND HARLOW

This book is dedicated to the
Master and Wardens and Court of Assistants
of the Worshipful Company
of Stationers and Newspaper Makers

AUTHOR'S NOTE

AN interest in printing should unite the most reverend biblio-grapher in the British Museum and the youngest apprentice in a back-street printer's shop, the sharp-witted account executive in the advertising agency and the library assistant working under less competitive pressure. In practice, any single group concerned with printing concentrates on its own aspect and regards the others with indifference; sometimes even with contempt.

There is one roof under which all can gather, and that is at St Bride's Institute, London, where the Technical Library is committed to serve everyone regardless of age, status or exper-ience. The text that follows was originally a series of lectures given at St Bride's, and in these lectures it was hoped to offer a common ground upon which could meet all the disparate units whose only links are the two words: 'printing' and 'London'. This was the considered policy of Mr Turner Berry, who was then the Librarian, inspired by the example of William Blades, whose own library is fundamental to the collection, for Blades was a practising master printer who also decisively contributed to scholarly studies. Mr Berry wished most, however, that the lec-tures should appeal to young people entering the trade, whether in publishing houses, agencies, journalism or the craft unions.

The effect of this purpose was an emphasis on certain incidents and personalities and a desire to interest rather than instruct. These traces have been left unmodified in the book, for there is instruction enough in the exciting resources of St Bride's to satisfy the most ardent. It was hoped also to encourage an interest in old books and newspapers for their own sake, not as specimens in a glass case, and with the co-operation of Mr Colin Richardson to demonstrate that one did not need a long purse to enter an antiquarian bookseller's. The lectures were given under the aegis of the University of London Extra-Mural Department.

With considerable fortitude, since he was already suffering from a painful spinal condition that laid him low for four months,

Mr Stanley Morison took the chair at the first meeting, and this was fitting for few men have had more at heart the wish to unite rather than divide those concerned with printing.

The substance of the lectures owes much to help from Mr Cyprian Blagden, Professor William Jackson and Mr Graham Pollard. Documented information on the development of the book trade has since been made public by Mr Pollard as the 1958-9 Sandars Lecturer in Bibliography, and Mr Blagden's history of the Stationers' Company is in the press. The text of the book has been extended following suggestions made by Mr Pollard.

Mr Charles Batey, who until October 1, 1958, was Printer to the University of Oxford, gave all possible assistance and hospitably allowed me access to the Constance Meade Collection at the University Press. Mrs Beatrice Warde, whose work for St Bride's in particular and for printing in general is an achievement without parallel, was eloquent in her encouragement. Mr S. H. Steinberg, whose book *Five Centuries of Printing* is indispensable, was another source of help. The Times Publishing Company gave an unstinted support only partly reflected by the number of illustrations here reproduced from negatives at Printing House Square.

I am also grateful to the present Director of the British Museum, to Professor Richmond P. Bond (University of North Carolina) and to Messrs M. H. Black (University Press, Cambridge), Harry Carter (University Press, Oxford), D. F. Foxon and A. F. Johnson (British Museum), K. A. Marshall (*The Times*), James Moran (*Printing News*), James Mosley (Librarian, St Bride's), J. C. T. Oates (University Library, Cambridge), the late George Westover (The Monotype Corporation Ltd.), and Berthold Wolpe (Faber & Faber). For permission to reproduce original material I thank the Governors of St Bride's Institute, the Printer to the University of Oxford, The Times Publishing Company, the Trustees of the British Museum, and the University Librarian, Cambridge, and for permission to refer to photostat records of the Stationers' Company I thank the Bibliographical Society and the Worshipful Company of Stationers and Newspaper Makers.

CONTENTS

CONTENTS

PLATES

———— ⟫✹⟪ ————

ILLUSTRATIONS IN TEXT

B

I

The Book Trade in
the Sixteenth Century

BOOKSELLING is a trade; honourable in itself and useful to learning. Printing is more than a trade. Practitioners in this country have long called it an 'art or mystery', reminding us that craftsmanship is involved at every stage of the reproduction and multiplication of the single original. It would be bold to describe printing in London as an art during much of the sixteenth and most of the seventeenth centuries, a period with which this book may seem overoccupied. But the printing produced in the latter half of the sixteenth century and main part of the seventeenth has been either overlooked or summarily dismissed by commentators on English typography. It is desirable that we brace ourselves to discover why this period has acquired its evil reputation, and how far that reputation is deserved.

Certainly, standards of typography and production declined from the middle of the sixteenth century. Was this due to some incapacity in the English to respect taste as well as utility? Or was it, as is commonly said, due to Government restriction?

The sixteenth-century book was much like its successor today. The basic principles of letterpress production are still the same: ink is spread over the raised surface of the type and an impression taken on a sheet of paper. The printed sheets are folded and bound in a traditional manner, though the process today has been partially mechanized. And a book still communicates the message of the author in the same way: the reader interprets the arrangement of alphabetical symbols. For that message the printer is not, and never has been, responsible: he is concerned only with the multiplication of copies.

The law in this country holds that the printer should concern himself with the subject-matter of the books that pass through his press if they are likely to be controversial, and the authorities in the sixteenth century showed towards the printing press a nervousness paralleled by the present-day control of other media of mass instruction. The entrenched position of the Lord Chamberlain's office as to plays and films and the attitude of the political parties as to television are obvious examples. The regulation of printed pornography is today as rigid as it has ever been and in most respects we have nothing like the freedom to libel that our ancestors enjoyed. In different degrees at different periods all Governments in this country, like Governments in other countries, have controlled printing and publishing. Why was it disastrous in sixteenth- and seventeenth-century London?

That there was strict control by the Government at that time cannot be denied; but to blame the Government for the deterioration in the style of typography and in the materials used obscures the problems that faced printers and booksellers. The two groups must be considered together for in the sixteenth century their relations were close. They were organized in a City livery company, the Company of Stationers,[1] since the description 'stationer' did not have so restricted a meaning as today. It could be applied to any member of the book trade—printer, bookseller or bookbinder—and was a word of considerable antiquity, deriving from a member of that trade who was in a fixed position as he would be at a stall or shop.

Long before printing was invented the centres of book production were the monasteries, where books were copied for Princes of the Church or State and for the use, education and edification of the clergy and a small body of laymen. During the rise in western Europe of the Universities, secular centres of book production were established and were thriving by the thirteenth century. Children needed schoolbooks and students needed textbooks so that in England by the mid-century a bespoke trade in books was commonplace in the two University towns and in London. The 'stationer' at a shop or stall would accept orders for a copy to be made by a scribe or writer, or he would hire out volumes which might be copied out before they were returned. In the shop or stall that handled this trade there were several craftsmen working in association: the man who prepared the parchment, then the scribe or writer, the illustrator or limner, the binder, and lastly, the man who acted as the business agent and took the orders and even sold parchment and quills, the man who has since become the stationer as we know him.

In the University towns the demand would be for editions of the classics and lawbooks. In London there would be school-masters needing elementary textbooks and grammars, and merchants and gentlemen who wanted books of devotion, romances, handbooks of sport and so on. Six hundred years ago, in 1357, the writers (copyists) of these books were sufficiently numerous to combine in a trade guild, together with, perhaps, the illustrators. This guild was the origin of the Stationers' Company. During the next two centuries it shed the writers who specialized in legal documents, brought in the bookbinders, and slowly came to include all those associated with the trade in written books.

It was essential to form this association, since no commodity could be sold in the City of London unless by a freeman of a livery company. The Stationers were a small and an insignificant company, sending only two representatives to the coronation of Richard III in 1483, whereas the great companies like the Mercers sent a dozen. The Stationers had their own livery, though they could not settle on the exact colour—it varied from violet to reddish purple to blood-red. So long as books were expensive and laborious to produce, the Stationers' Company were likely to remain small and insignificant.

Was Caxton a member of the Stationers' Company? He was not. It was not the Stationers who introduced printing into this country: the process was as much a novelty to them as to anyone else. Caxton was a prominent member of the Mercers' Company, who decided to set up his printing house in the precincts of Westminster Abbey, in the neighbourhood of Parliament and—then—of the Law Courts, where he secured a market for both secular and religious books. Later printers moved eastwards to tap the rich market of the City of London.

There was no hostility on the part of the Stationers. Too many of them were alert to the advantages of printing. The booksellers could appreciate the value of an invention which made possible the rapid duplication of books: they saw the possibility of drastic reductions in price and an infinite increase in trade. Those members of the Company who were binders saw the prospect of more work than they had ever known. Only the writers and the limners faced a problem somewhat similar to that which automation is thought to offer today. For a time the limners were employed in rubricating books—in some early printed books every capital letter has been touched up with colour. The writers were employed by those who preferred the hand-produced article: court poets, for example, circulated their poems in manuscript, and many small documents that today would be printed continued to be produced by hand. These craftsmen appear to have been absorbed into the book trade or into other trades without hardship.

The readiness of the booksellers, the binders and, for a time, the limners, to accept and participate in the new invention, eased the relationship between the Company and the printers. The records are, unfortunately, missing that would show the steps by which they were reconciled; but the identity of economic interests and other pressures are clear enough. When the charter was granted in 1557 to the Stationers' Company, the booksellers and the printers were the dominant group, and the original members, the limners and writers, were not involved.[2]

This excursion into history recalls how the Stationers' Company came into existence. More important, it recalls the forgotten books of the trade: schoolbooks, textbooks, lawbooks and editions of the classics—the books that were not the principal concern of the monastic scriptoria, the books for which demand was so great that a trade guild came into existence.

But Caxton printed none of these books. His titles fall into two chief groups: books of devotion and light reading matter. He printed no Bibles, he printed no textbooks. His general publishing policy was to print, usually in English, books that were unlikely to be imported. He concentrated on such works as the *Book of Hours* used at Salisbury Cathedral and elsewhere in this country, or on Chaucer's *Canterbury Tales*.[3] It was his successor, Wynkyn de Worde, who saw that there would be also a market for textbooks, particularly lawbooks, and he adapted his former master's publishing policy to include these subjects—to his profit.[4]

Caxton was a businessman, understanding the necessity for small 'jobs' that could be quickly executed, such as the Indulgence printed before December 13, 1476, which is the first datable piece of London printing, and he was alive to the value of advertising (see p. 173). But, making his own translations, he was something of a scholar and an individualist as well as a craftsman and tradesman: he printed what he liked. Wynkyn de Worde was the more hard-headed man of business. He saw that the invention had made possible the rapid multiplication of standard texts that were in everyday use: the titles that had once been the economic prop of a flourishing trade guild.

De Worde and his contemporaries of the incunable period—John Lettou, John Barbier, William de Machlinia, Julian Notary, Richard Pynson—these men bent their energies to supply the insatiable demand from students and schoolmasters, lawyers and laymen, who had once supported the manuscript book trade. The output of Lettou, Machlinia, Barbier and Notary appears small when we catalogue what has survived. But many of their editions may have fallen to pieces through constant use. The romance of *Godfrey of Boloyne*, printed by Caxton, may have sat on the bookshelf like a set of Jane Austen and been lovingly read once a year; but a legal yearbook may have been consulted every day until its pages disintegrated.

During the reign of Henry VII and the first years of Henry VIII, when these printers were at work, the English Renaissance was proceeding, and it was natural for London printers to set the works of English scholars. So Pynson published Colet and Linacre, and William Rastell published Sir Thomas More, and someone, possibly De Worde, published in or after 1509 the *Rudimenta* of William Lillie, later to be expanded into 'Lillie's' Latin Grammar, the book that was to be a best-seller for two centuries, but of which very few copies indeed survive out of the million or more that were printed in that period.[5]

Nevertheless, the world of learning was international, and reliance upon imported books was as inevitable in the early days of London printing as reliance upon foreign-born craftsmen and imported materials. Only when a generation of English apprentices reached maturity between 1515 and 1520 did the trade begin to expand and to seek protection from foreign competition. The Act of Parliament of 1484 that had permitted foreigners to trade in books and foreign craftsmen to work in this country was repealed. After 1523 successive Acts restricted the activities of foreigners until they were entirely excluded. Printing in London

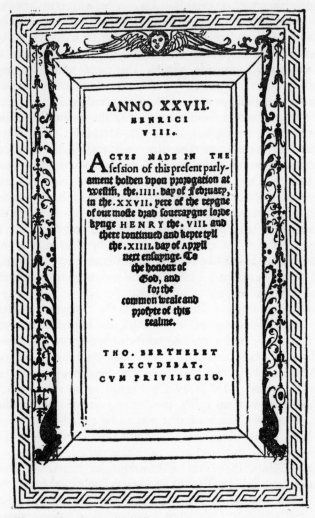

Fig. 1. 8⅜ × 5⅛ in., including frame.

may be said to have come of age in 1535 when a native of this country, Thomas Berthelet (Welsh by birth), printed the first Bible—which was, incidentally, the last Vulgate to be printed in London.

Berthelet was a careful printer and a conscientious typographer. Like his predecessors, he produced many law-books. The title page of the *Acts* 27 Henry VIII (Fig. 1) is typical of its period in the use of the frame, although this particular design was unusual, and one would not be surprised to find it on a Pre-Raphaelite title-page. It came from France, but was not copied by Berthelet's contemporaries, whereas his triangular arrangment of the type-matter was continually imitated.[6]

In an Act of 1534 it was explicitly stated that there were then in England 'a great number cunning and expert in the science of printing'. But for many years before, there had been enough printers for competition to begin. Certain titles sold much better than others. Lawbooks were an example. And as soon as a work was likely to be a best-seller it was likely to be pirated. When a printer had gone to the trouble of obtaining a manuscript and had, like Berthelet, set it up with care and procured good white paper, he wished, naturally, to have the sole profits. These would be diminished with every copy sold by another printer. The problem of protecting copyright arose as soon as there were any number— let alone a great number—'cunning and expert' in printing.

Since the Stationers' Company was an ineffective instrument until the printers joined it in force, the problem of protecting rights in a title was first solved by invoking the royal prerogative. Thus, about 1520—more than a decade before the Berthelet law-book—there is this imprint:

Cͫ Empꝛyntyd in Londoñ on ꝥ foͧth fyde of paulys by Iohñ Raftell with ꝥ ꝓiuylege of our moft futferaiyn loꝛd kyng Henry the. viii. grauntyd to the cͦmpyler therof · that noo man in thys hys realme fell none but fuch as the faine cͦpyler makyth pꝛyn⸗ tyd foꝛ ꝥ fpace of ii. yeere.

Fig. 2

In this case, the compiler was the scholar Thomas Linacre, but in general the author had no rights in his own work, these royal privileges being usually obtained by the printers and booksellers.[7]

So long an announcement was likely to be contracted and soon there appeared the simpler form: 'With the privilege of the King, *cum privilegio regali*', with no time limit mentioned. It was not in the interest of the printers and booksellers that there should be a time limit—the dream of perpetual copyright is an old one. Later, the phrase was emended to the familiar 'with the privilege of printing only', *cum privilegio ad imprimendum solum*. The emendation appeared during the 1530s when it became apparent that the royal privilege was being applied to books, the contents of which were too controversial for the King to approve at a period when he was obtaining his divorce from Catherine of Aragon and shaking off the authority of the Pope. Thus, by a Proclamation of 1538 all books had to be licensed as fit before they were published.

This requirement that all books should be licensed was the first intervention of government that was to the disadvantage of the trade. On the other hand, the sole right of the printer or bookseller to the title was still protected by the privilege. The licensing was a nuisance to printers, who evaded it when they could. In other matters the interest of the government coincided to a striking degree with the interest of the trade. Both were eager to control the importation of books—though for different reasons. The printers and booksellers wanted to eliminate sources of competition, the Government to eliminate sources of sedition. Both needs became acute as the century advanced. It was in the interest of both parties that the printers and booksellers should be organized in a single body that would be the instrument to accomplish their common ends. There had to be an assembly representative of the trade that could negotiate, enforce and petition.

In 1557 the Company of Stationers was granted its royal charter, by which Queen Mary gave its membership of printers and booksellers the sole right to publish books that secured a licence. They were also given the right to search out unlicensed printing and imported literature. The quater-centenary of this charter was handsomely celebrated on June 3, 1957; it is doubtful if those rejoicungs were more than a pale shadow of the exuberance with which the original printers and booksellers expressed their joy on the day of incorporation. There were then only one hundred-odd members. But thirty-one gallons of wine went into Stationers' Hall, a barrel of strong beer, another of double beer and a stand of ale. The food was no less lavish—twenty gallons of cream disappeared down the hundred-odd throats. The veal, mutton, capon, geese, venison and chicken pies, the cherries and gooseberries, were eaten by printers and booksellers who were decked with garlands and refreshed by musicians and perfume. They had something to celebrate: the charter meant that these hundred-odd men controlled the whole printing and bookselling trade.[8]

By the constitution of the Company, rule was in the hands of the Master and two Wardens, elected annually, and the Assistants, some eight to twelve senior members—a constitution usual in City companies. These officials met frequently but irregularly at a Court held in Stationers' Hall, where disputes were settled and ordinances promulgated. The non-governing body of the company consisted of the liverymen and the freemen or yeomen, the latter being fully trained men who could become liverymen—be clothed, the expression was—if they wished, by presentation and payment. It became the practice in the Stationers' Company to co-opt Assistants from the livery, and the yeomen did not even have a voice in the election of the Master and Wardens.[9]

The use dwindled of the protective imprint, *cum privilegio ad imprimendum solum.* Titles of which only one edition was envisaged were entered after licensing in a register at Stationers' Hall, a small fee, 4d at first, being paid. The titles then became the 'copies' of the man who entered them, and he alone had the right to publish them. Such 'copies' could be sold, and often were.

The most discerning printers and booksellers recognized that it would be more advantageous to secure a privilege relating to a class of books rather than to individual titles. Thus, Richard Tottel secured all lawbooks, John Day the ABC and Catechism, William Seres all books of private prayer, and so on. These were the books that brought in the profits. They were also the books that were likely to be pirated.[10]

Before investigating the affairs of the Stationers' Company in the sixteenth century a typical Stationer might be investigated. Henry Bynneman was a master printer, and a successful one, with two shops in St Paul's Churchyard and two houses in Upper

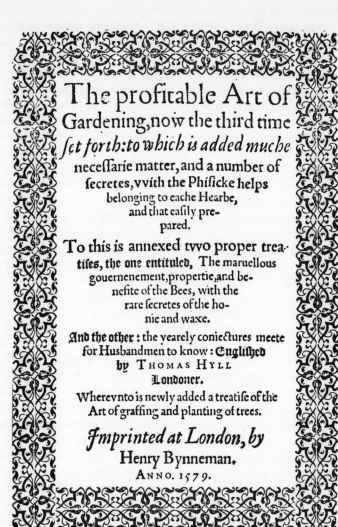

The profitable Art of
Gardening, now the third time
set forth: to which is added muche
necessarie matter, and a number of
secretes, vvith the Phisicke helps
belonging to eache Hearbe,
and that easily pre-
pared.

To this is annexed tvvo proper trea-
tises, the one entituled, The maruellous
gouernenement, propertie, and be-
nefite of the Bees, with the
rare secretes of the ho-
nie and waxe.

And the other : the yearely coniectures meete
for Husbandmen to know : Englished
by THOMAS HYLL
Londoner.

Wherevnto is newly added a treatise of the
Art of graffing and planting of trees.

Imprinted at London, by
Henry Bynneman.
ANNO. 1579.

Fig. 3. 6 × 4$\frac{1}{16}$ in., including border.

Thames Street, near St Benet, Paul's wharf. Bynneman was not, however, a leading Stationer, not a member of the Court— merely a substantial liveryman with great competence in his trade. A typical title-page is shown at Fig. 3. It is well laid out— the Elizabethans saw nothing undesirable in word-breaking; the presswork is adequate; the arabesque ornament is used with skill. On other title-pages the outside edges are not straight but arranged in scallops, like a lace-fringed cloth, and within the text Bynneman would recompose the units to make attractive tailpieces.[11]

It is easy to imagine the appearance of the printing house in which such a title-page was produced. As to the outside, it would be similar to those still overhanging the pavement at Temple Bar, London, or elsewhere in the country. Within, the small rooms would be low-ceilinged, rather dark, and likely to be seem overfull when a printing press was installed, for the wooden hand press might be six feet high or more (see Plate 1). We know something of Bynneman's possessions, since an inventory was taken after his death in 1583—five years before the Armada.[12] The premises cannot have been warm; he had only one pair of tongs and one fire-shovel. He was an ardent royalist, with two framed portraits of Queen Elizabeth that were worth more than much of his furniture. He had quite a wardrobe; the frieze jerkin and a white striped doublet were probably his working clothes, but he had others more splendid: a gown faced with damask and welted with velvet, a doublet of changeable grosgrain trimmed with lace, a black cloak faced with taffeta—and, of course, his livery. He liked pictures, for he had seven in chalk, five others and two uniden-tified portraits, as well as a map of the world. But his most endearing possession was, perhaps, his song-bird.

The cast type in Bynneman's establishment is not separately listed but is included in a general entry of 'printing stuff, cases, metal letter and other things', valued at £84, a considerable sum. The 'other things' may have included metal decorated initials, factotums, arabesque ornaments. His Hebrew and Greek types were, however, entered: 30 lb. of Hebrew in its case, 60 lb. of Greek, and the two valued at 37s 6d. The values, incidentally, are likely to be underestimates.

Bynneman had a collection of matrices valued at over £12 of which the Hebrew was by far the most valuable at £3. In his possession of this face Bynneman was untypical of London printers: he had recently bought it in preparation for a Hebrew dictionary. He had only two sizes of italic, one—perhaps large—valued at 26s 8d, whereas a roman—perhaps small—was valued at only 6s 8d. The set of matrices for secretary, a calligraphic face, was valued at 50s, and probably worth them, for such a script must have been a punch-cutter's nightmare. His set of 'diverse sorts' may be the matrices for ornament or initials: these are not otherwise mentioned. Just before his death a special 'vignette' had been cut for the dictionaries he planned, value 6s 8d.

The value of the composing side of the house far exceeded that of the press side. Bynneman was fortunate in that he was working before the master printers were restricted in the number of presses they might own, and so he was able to have three, later the prerogative of officials of the Company. The furniture, unfortunately, is another of the inclusive entries: it and the presses were valued at £13 6s 8d, almost certainly an underestimate, for later second-hand presses were worth £10 each.

Bynneman was not only a printer but a publisher and book-seller, with an immense stock of volumes on his hands, some in editions printed many years before. Thus, he had 125 copies of Virgil's *Eclogues*, printed eleven years earlier than the date of the inventory. Though Bynneman had specialized in the provision of annotated classical texts for use in the upper forms of grammar schools, books hitherto imported, the inventory shows a variety of titles. It is odd that he could not dispose more quickly of such titles as the *Murder of G. Saunders* (1577, 350 copies left in 1583) or *The Discourse of the Great Cruelty of a Widow Towards a Young Gentleman*. The latter dated from 1570, when Bynneman had been a liveryman for only three years. But it was in verse and was, perhaps, intolerable—the first sentence of the author's (prose) address to the reader runs to over eighty words.[13]

The handbook on gardening had sold well, but it is clear from the inventory that titles such as *A Persuasion from Papistry* or *The Stage of Popish Toys* moved most quickly. Out of a possible edition of 1,000 or 1,500, Bynneman had about thirty of each left, though both had been recently published. In all, he had stocks ranging from a score to nearly a thousand books of over eighty titles. This represents considerable capital tied up over a long period. The inventory was taken because Bynneman was being

sued for repayment of £1,000 he had borrowed; the entire value
of the estate came to less than this sum.

Before his death Bynneman may have taken a more hopeful
view. First, he had the sole right to print many of the eighty-odd
titles that he stocked, since they were entered to him in the
register at Stationers' Hall, and he therefore held the copyright.
Secondly, he had the privilege granted in 1580 of printing 'all
dictionaries in all tongues, all chronicles and histories whatsoever'. This privilege he appears to have been preparing vigorously to exercise, and had borrowed the thousand pounds, no
doubt, for this purpose. Work on two dictionaries was so far
advanced that they were published in the year after his death.

Cooper's Latin-English dictionary was equal, typographically,
to anything produced by the celebrated John Day. It is a folio
volume with a well-executed, if restrained, title-page (see Fig. 4).
The vignette may be the 6s 8d one that had been specially cut. The
presswork is good—even remarkably good, since the bulk of the
book is in small type. In the preliminaries Bynneman used some
fine initial letters about two inches square, carefully fitted into
the text (see Fig. 5). The final page carries two large ornaments,
and though both are attractive, either one on its own would have
been sufficient—Bynneman's executors, who completed the
work, may have lacked his taste.

The other dictionary of 1584 was Morelius' Greek-Latin-
English, which was assigned to his creditor who may thus have
received his thousand pounds. The privilege itself was bought by
two Stationers, which probably accounts for the widow's later
possession of an estate of £300-£500.

It is clear that Bynneman himself was enthusiastic about his
dictionary privilege. Not only had he invested borrowed money
in new equipment, but he had re-orientated his printing policy
so that he could execute the privilege. He had stripped his cases
of the many decorative ornaments he had been accustomed to
hold, and reduced the number of sizes that he held of roman and
italic founts. He had lost interest in his 'copies'—wisely, perhaps,
since the editions already stocked appear to have satisfied demand.
Bynneman's attitude towards his privilege was typical of printers of
that time, and illustrates the importance attached to these comprehensive privileges which played so great a part in the affairs of
the Stationers' Company until the end of the seventeenth century.

THESAVRVS LINGVÆ

Romanæ & Britannicæ, tam accurate congeſtus,
vt nihil penè in eo deſyderari poſsit, quod vel Latinè complecta-
tur ampliſsimus Stephani Theſaurus, vel Anglicè, toties aucta Eliotæ Biblio-
theca : opera & induſtria Thomæ Cooperi Magdalenenſis.

Quid fructus ex hoc Theſauro ſtudioſi poſsint excerpere, & quam rationem
ſecutus author ſit in Vocabulorum interpretatione & diſpoſi-
tione, poſt epiſtolam demonſtratur.

*ACCESSIT DICTIONARIVM HISTO-
ricum & poëticum propria vocabula Virorum, Mulierum,
Sectarum, Populorum, Vrbium, Montium, & cæterorum
locorum complectens, & in his iucundiſsimas & omnium cogni-
tione digniſsimas hiſtorias.*

In Theſaurum Thomæ Cooperi Magdalenenſis,
hexaſtichon Richardi Stephani.

Vileſcæ rutila diues Pactôlus arena,
  Hermus,& auriferi nobilis vnda Tagi.
Vileſcant Crœſi gemmæ,Midæque talenta:
  Maior apud Britones eruta gaza patet.
Hoc Wainflete tuo gens Anglica debet alumno,
  Qui vigili nobis tanta labore dedit.

Impreſſum Londini.
1584.

Fig. 4. Thomas Cooper's Latin-English
Dictionary printed by Bynneman.
Page size $12\frac{1}{2} \times 8\frac{1}{4}$ in.

AD CLARISSIMVM VIRVM

Robertum Dudleium, Leiceſtriæ Comitem,

Regiæ maieſtati à conſilijs, & Oxonienſis Academiæ Cancellarium, Thomæ Cooperi, de
Theſauri dedicatione, epiſtola.

VM ſuperioribus annis (illuſtriſſime vir) in ſubſidium
ſtudioſæ iuuentutis Eliota Dictionarium Latino an-
glicum maximis laboribus conficeret: mihi viſus eſt
vir doctus & prudēs mente cogitationéq; proſpexiſſe,
in quantas anguſtias ætate ſubſequente res literaria
prolapſura videretur. Poſtquam enim noſtra memo-
ria, propter graues temporum & religionis mutatio-
nes, antiſtites Eccleſiæ verbiq; miniſtri, non in contemptum modò hominum, ſed in periculum etiam ſa-
lutis & fortunarum trahi cœperunt: mirum profectò
quam ex eo tempore quotidie magis deiecta ſit iuuentutis ſpes & induſtria,
quam vbique contemptæ iacuerint artes & diſciplinæ. Nam cum illud vitæ ge-
nus, cuius antea dignitas & amplitudo quaſi præmium ſtudioſorum laboribus
propoſitum fuit, iam vel, quod multi putant, coniunctam habeat ignominiam,
vel, quod impij ſperant, imminentem calamitatem: & parentes, ſuorum proſpi-
cientes commodis, alia vitæ inſtituta liberis præſcribunt: & ipſi iuuenes, vulgi
potius exiſtimationem quam rerum dignitatē ſequentes, ad quiduis ſunt promp-
tiores, quam ad diuturnas ſtudiorum moleſtias ſine certo fructu perferendas.
Hinc itaque fit, quod à præclaris ingenijs præmaturè diſtituantur Academiæ &
ſcholæ publicæ, multoſq; iuuenes habeant liberaliter ſanè inſtitutos educatione
doctrinaq; puerili, ſed paucos admodum, qui cognitionis & ſcientiæ cupidi, in li-
teras illas interiores & reconditas altius penetrare ſtudeant: niſi qui fortè ad me-
dicinæ cognitionem, aut iuriſprudentiam paulo maiori impetu ferantur. Reliqui,
vel abiectis ſtudijs ad aulicam vitam confugiunt, vel ad regni inſtituta ediſcenda
ſe conferunt, vel ad alias ætatis degendæ rationes deſciſcunt, ex quibus amplio-
res credunt vtilitates ſibi profecturas. Quamobrem meritò mihi videntur con-
queri Chriſtianæ religionis præſides & viri doctiſſimi, quibus eiuſdem hodie tra-
dita eſt adminiſtratio, cum incredibili veritatis Euangelicæ incommodo magnam
eſſe in pleriſq; locis eccleſiarum, deſtitutionem, ſummamq; penuriam eorum, qui
diuini fœderis præconium ſuſcipiant, qui Eccleſiaſtica munia ſubeant, qui reli-
quas literatæ pietatis functiones exerceant. Cum enim cæteras reipublicæ par-
tes capeſcentibus certi honores magnaq; præmia proponantur, Eccleſiarum ve-
rò rectoribus & literarum magiſtris ad contemptum maior quàm ad laudem lo-
cus relictus ſit: non mirum ſi multi reperiantur, qui gloriam & dignitatem, pauci
qui cuniunctam cum ignominia virtutem & doctrinam perſequantur. Sed im-
prudenter à me & intempeſtiuè hæc illata videtur querela, cum omnium iam
ſermone peruulgatum ſit, tuo maxime conſilio, & clariſſimi viri Sicilli maieſtatem
Regiam iamdudum inijſſe rationem, quemadmodum non artes ſolum iniuria
temporis labantes in priſtinam reſtituantur dignitatem, ſed etiam vt iuuentus
ignauia langueſcens gloriæ ſtimulis erecta magis conſtanter perferat graues ſtu-
¶.3.

diorum

Fig. 5. A page from the preliminaries
of Cooper's Dictionary.

C

Bynneman's 'copies' include none of the titles that were obvious and sure best-sellers, such as grammar books, ABCs, Bibles, Prayer Books or the *Acts and Monuments* of John Foxe, the martyrologist (see Plate III). Such books would go through edition after edition year after year. Every literate person who could afford them would buy them. But Bynneman's titles were those that might be bought only when a man had pennies to spare. Few of them reached a second edition.

Here we have the crux of publishing policy in the sixteenth and seventeenth centuries. The sure best-sellers were all protected by privileges. Bynneman could never publish them. He had come late on the scene. All the most profitable lines were in the hands of others. He was pleased to have his dictionary privilege, but it was not one of the best. The greatest privilege printer of all, the holder of the Bible patent, wrote a shrewd account of the various privileges, and he declared that the heavy investment demanded in stock and equipment was a serious drawback to that for dictionaries.[14] Bynneman had discovered the truth of this statement, and even today dictionary publishing is a limited field.

Other privileges were more easily exercised. Richard Tottel, who printed all lawbooks, had built up his business gradually on the basis laid by Berthelet and his contemporaries. John Day, rightly celebrated by Updike for his typography, had the ABC, the Psalms in Metre and the Catechism. William Seres, once his partner, had books of devotion. Richard Watkins had almanacs. A syndicate in which the Norton family finally ousted its partners had the grammar. Christopher Barker, the Queen's Printer, had the Bible, the Book of Common Prayer, Acts of Parliament and Royal Proclamations. All these men were powerful in the Company, Tottell being Master twice, Seres no fewer than five times. Their privileges brought them power.

At least three of the privileged printers were powerful because they held books of religion or basic education. Had John Day, one of the richest Stationers, been asked which he considered his most valuable properties—and had he given a truthful answer— he would have said that Foxe's *Martyrs*, the ABC and the Psalms in Metre were the prop of his fortune.

The Psalms were those often referred to as the 'Singing Psalms' or as 'Sternhold and Hopkins'. They were metrical, unlike those

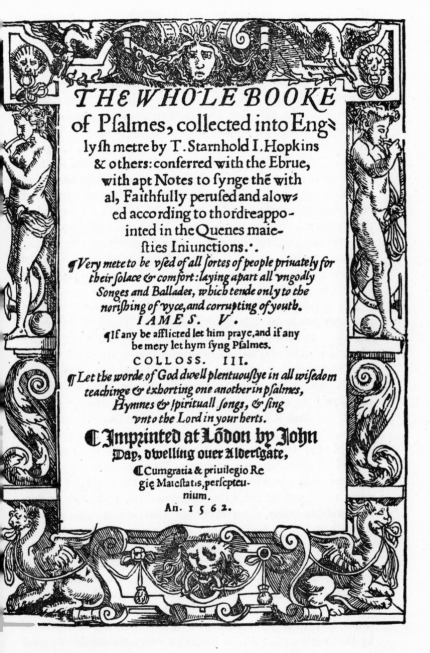

THE WHOLE BOOKE

of Pſalmes, collected into Eng
lyſh metre by T. Starnhold I. Hopkins
& others: conferred with the Ebrue,
with apt Notes to ſynge thē with
al, Faithfully peruſed and alow
ed according to thordreappo-
inted in the Quenes maie-
ſties Iniunctions.

❡ Very mete to be vſed of all ſortes of people priuately for
their ſolace & comfort: laying apart all vngodly
Songes and Ballades, which tende only to the
noriſhing of vyce, and corrupting of youth.

IAMES. V.

❡ If any be afflicted let him praye, and if any
be mery let hym ſyng Pſalmes.

COLLOSS. III.

❡ Let the worde of God dwell plentuouſlye in all wiſedom
teachinge & exhorting one another in pſalmes,
Hymnes & ſpirituall ſongs, & ſing
vnto the Lord in your herts.

❡ Imprinted at Lōdon by John
Day, dwelling ouer Aldersgate,

❡ Cumgratia & priuilegio Re
gię Maiestatis, perſcpteu-
nium.

An. 1 5 6 2.

Fig. 6. Page size 12¼ × 7¾ in.

in the Book of Common Prayer, which were and still are from the translation made for Henry VIII's Great Bible, and not primarily intended to be sung. In Elizabeth's reign church-going was compulsory. Yet, although the Elizabethans loved to sing, there were no hymns and they had to rely on the psalms for their tuneful worship. So the effort of Thomas Sternhold—a groom of the chamber to Henry VIII—to provide a version fit for the voice was greeted with enthusiasm. His work was continued after Elizabeth became Queen by John Hopkins. In 1562 Day printed the final edition of the joint version, and in the following year an edition with four-part settings. Thus, the Singing Psalms were launched on a career of extraordinary success which lasted until the end of the eighteenth century, when hymnbooks came into general use. For over two hundred years one or more editions of the Singing Psalms appeared annually, a record paralleled by few books other than the Bible and the Book of Common Prayer, the Catechism and the 'Lillie' grammar.[15]

The importance of the ABC as a source of profit when its publisher holds the sole right is obvious. Since Day possessed also the Catechism, he held the monopoly of books of primary education—it is only in modern times that every child has not been required to learn the Catechism. These two productions, usually bound together, and the third, the Singing Psalms, would be bought by every household where one member had the first of the three R's. When the children went on to the grammar school, they would be taught from the 'Lillie' Latin grammar. The Norton family never relaxed their efforts to obtain sole control of this lucrative property. To give some idea of the printing orders involved in such properties: at a later period, when a contract for the 'Lillie' grammar was made with an outside printing house, the number was 3,000 a year. This was at a time when a normal edition of a book, perhaps printed only the once, was rarely more than 1,500.[16]

Like the Catechism and the Singing Psalms, the books of private prayer controlled by William Seres are no longer important; but in sixteenth and seventeenth centuries they were bestsellers, and Seres had also the right to the primer. In Catholic times the primer had been a book of devotion, and as continued by the Anglican Church, it became a necessary household book at a period when family prayers were held every morning and evening. In theory, the Anglican primer was distinct from the Book of Common Prayer, though Seres—in the spirit typical of Elizabethan publishing—began to insert bits of the morning and evening service so that, according to the Queen's Printer, sales of the Book of Common Prayer were diminished.

Many of these private prayers were far removed from those that saints and mystics might have used. The list of contents forms an enlightening commentary upon the objects of prayer that lay closest to the Elizabethan heart. Beside the 'sundry godly prayers' for the Queen, as were proper, there were those for gentlemen, landlords, merchants, rich men, poor men, maidens, wives, single men, households and all Christians: a list which nicely limns the class distinctions of that day. Another section provided prayers for specific virtues, among them charity, humility, which cannot be faulted. But there were other petitions, in prosperity, to stay in it and, in adversity, to get out of it, which evoke the unspiritual picture of a whole Elizabethan family on its knees imploring the Almighty for what was described to him as 'a competent living'.[17]

In early times Seres had taken the trouble to print his books of devotion in red and black and to produce an attractive volume of small pocket format. But later no time was found for niceties, so great were the printing orders. Many prayer books were compiled by divines and private persons: *The Castle of Comfort*, *The Sick Man's Salve* and *A Pomander of Prayer* by Thomas Becon, *The Diamond of Devotion* (Abraham Fleming), *The Seven Sobs of a Sorrowful Soul for Sin* (William Hunnis)—alliterative titles were much favoured. Seres could not possibly print all these himself, but he claimed the right to do so under his privilege, and when 'great suit and debate at law' were threatened as the consequence of seventeen members of the Company claiming titles as their 'copy', Seres managed to bulldoze everyone into an agreement whereby he received a shilling for each impression printed outside his own office. The most popular titles went through an impression every two or three years.[18]

The almanac was another valuable privilege. There were formats that resembled the modern diary, but it was the single sheet that brought in the cash, for it was cheap and had to be bought afresh each year. The 'prognostications' included were weather forecasts and astronomical data, accompanied by a

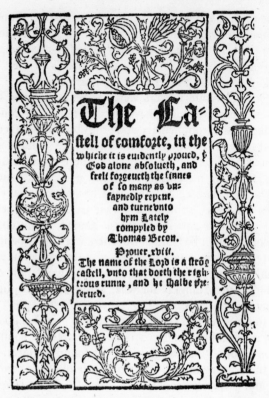

The La-
ſtell of comfoȝte, in the
whiche it is euidently pꝛoued, ꝑ
God alone abſoluceth, and
frelt foꝛgeueth the ſinnes
of ſo many as vn=
faynedly repent,
and turne vnto
hym Lately
compyled by
Thomas Becon.

Pꝛouer.rviii.
The name of the Loꝛd is a ſtrõg
caſtell, vnto that doeth the righ-
tious runne, and he ſhalbe pꝛe-
ſerued.

Fig. 7.
Page size
$5\frac{1}{4} \times 3\frac{1}{2}$ in.

woodcut of the astronomical man, showing which parts of the body were ruled by what signs of the zodiac. When Sir Toby Belch said of Taurus 'that's legs and thighs', he may have been thinking of the almanac's little block.[19]

Among the privileged printers was the Queen's Printer, who is described in Chapter III. His patent included the Bible, the Book of Common Prayer, Statutes and Proclamations, as well as smaller properties.

Thus, nearly all the books likely to be in everyday use throughout the kingdom were the monopolies of a few men. Their supremacy did not go unchallenged. A bold spirit, John Wolfe, formerly apprenticed to Day, declared that 'just as Luther had reformed religion', so he would reform the government of the printing and bookselling trades. He began to print what he pleased, regardless of privilege, and found a few supporters

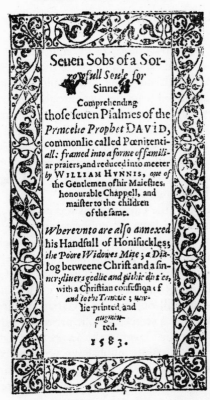

Fig. 8.
Page size
$4\frac{7}{16} \times 2\frac{1}{2}$ in.

Wolfe was a remarkable man, who deserves honour for other achievements (see p. 109) even if in this matter his motives were not exactly pure.[20]

His rebellion had this effect: that the privileged printers agreed to resign their rights to certain 'copies'—not, of course, the best —for the benefit of the Company's poor. Wolfe was bought off by being allowed to share in Day's privilege. He was given the sheet of the ABC that went under the transparent window of the hornbook, a valuable property since every child began with a hornbook, but easily pirated, being a small, single sheet (see Plate II*b*). [21] To add bulk, Day preferred to print the Catechism with the ABC, and he showed a typical shrewdness when he let Wolfe have the most vulnerable of the 'small copies'.

It was easy to pirate a book, particularly one already published, since the compositor merely set from the printed text. The pirate could be stopped by making it impossible for him to obtain type or press, and that the Company did, with the help of the Government. But if the pirate had the equipment it was necessary to be able to enter his shop and to seize the impression before it could be sent out. Although the charter allowed the Company to seek out unauthorized printing, the officials appear to have been reluctant to rely upon the charter alone in this matter. They may have feared public resentment at entry and seizure, for no one is so touchy as the Englishman whose house is his castle. Yet these were the only means by which copy or privilege could be protected, and so the Company was eager to seek legal warrant to make restrictive ordinances.

During the 1580s the Government was no less eager to restrict the trade. There had been the publications, viewed as seditious, of the Puritan, John Stubbs, who had been condemned to have his right hand cut off—when this had been done, he lifted the left, pulled off his cap and cried 'God save the Queen!' There were other Puritans no less obstinate, no less loyal. But the Government was still opposed to sectarian publications. There was also in existence a secret Catholic press, publishing literature that in the eyes of the Government was equally seditious.

These illicit if disparate publishing ventures coincided with John Wolfe's rebellion against the privileged printers. With a skill characteristic of the time, he took advantage of disturbed conditions to make a profitable bargain for himself. But the Company had no intention of encouraging a John Wolfe to abuse the vested interests of owners of copyrights. Nor had the Government the intention to encourage a John Stubbs to abuse the hierarchy of the Anglican Church. It suited both parties that the number of master printers should be limited, the number of presses and apprentices held to a minimum and entry and seizure enforced. Regulations to this effect were decreed from the Star Chamber at Westminster in 1586.

The interest of the Company in this Star Chamber decree can be traced. Two years before it was issued, the Stationers had decided to enforce their own ordinances as to search and seizure. The elders of the Company were consulted by the Privy Council before the decree was framed. After it was published, the privileged printers met at Stationers' Hall. These rich men gathered —close-fisted like most rich men, ready to argue when obligations were due or when they were fined for misdemeanours—and yet, although their legal adviser had received generous fees, they insisted on a whip-round, to which one and all contributed fivers, which were then worth nearly ten times what they are today. So much did the Star Chamber regulations lighten their hearts.[22]

At once the officials of the Company began to carry out searches and they showed most eagerness in hunting down those who were pirating grammars and almanacs and such 'copies'. For example, in the October after the decree was issued two searches were made. One was recorded briefly, and possibly concerned seditious printing. The other was described in detail: the wretched pirate had been found with the grammar in octavo, the primer, the psalter calendar and 'certain other formes ready set with other men's copies'. The indignation thereby roused rings in the report.[23] This was the great crime in the eyes of the Company: the printing of other men's copies.

The punishment of such offenders was loss of their presses and type. The former would be broken and the latter defaced. Never were presses or type put up for sale. That would have defeated the Company's object: to make printing equipment difficult to obtain. When the offence was mild, the offender had to part with the bar of his press until he would give an undertaking to conform.

The Star Chamber decree also reaffirmed the licensing system. This affected new copies but not the privileged books, which merely went through edition after edition, too familiar for the licensers to be concerned with them. The whole story of the privileges, the reactions of the Company as revealed in the records, the participation of the Company in the framing of the decree and their conduct after its publication: all confirm the desperate need of the powerful Stationers to protect their properties. The policy of the printers and booksellers was hardened in a mould not to be broken for more than a century.

In addition to the Star Chamber decree of 1586 there was another event which exerted a far-reaching effect upon the trade: the death in 1584 of John Day. Some time before his death he had taken partners, both because he could not himself easily wield his vast aggregation of privileges and because partners were desirable in order to secure an interest within the Company in the protection of his copies. Partnerships were not unusual in the trade, but it was inevitable that the value of Day's properties should attract the most influential men in the Company. After his death his son appears to have welcomed participation, and in 1594, a decade later, there were seventeen partners. Who were they? The Court of Assistants was, almost certainly, there in full strength: eleven of the partners were Assistants, and this would have been the entire Court at that time.[24]

A machinery to administer the privileges had been set up with a treasurer and two stock-keepers. Further, Seres' privilege had been reconstructed in the same way and with the same people participating, and the two partnerships were thereafter associated and referred to as a joint enterprise.

Thus, the decisions on the conduct of Day's properties were being taken by the governing body of the Company. This had happened naturally. The need for protection and partnership was genuine and the final evolution had been due to Richard Day's lack of the energy and devotion to business that had so marked his father. He was content to allow others to share with him, and indeed to control, what had become a printing empire.

This economic development held great risks for the Company. It is always undesirable that members of a governing body should have an economic interest unshared by those they govern. The temptation to fiddle is thought to be more than human nature can resist. Today, members of Parliament, for example, are protected from temptation: they must not take offices of profit under the Crown. The seventeenth century revealed the risks inherent when the book trade was controlled by a group of men not unaccustomed to pray daily to be permitted to remain in a state of prosperity.

NOTES

1 Graham Pollard, 'The Company of Stationers before 1557', *The Library* (June 1937), xviii, 1.

2 E. Arber, *Transcript of the Registers of the Company of Stationers, 1554-1640* (London, 1875-1894, 5 vols.), i, p. xxxiii, prints a list of the members in 1557.

3 George Bullen, *Catalogue of the Caxton Exhibition* (1877).

4 H. R. Plomer, *Wynkyn de Worde and His Contemporaries* (London, 1925).

5 C. G. Allen, 'The Sources of "Lily's Latin Grammar": A Review of the Facts and some further suggestions', *The Library* (1954), ix, 85.

6 John Bagford collected a number of Berthelet's title-pages. B.M. Harl. MSS., 5928.

7 A. W. Reed, 'The Regulation of the Book Trade before the Proclamation of 1538', Trans. Bib. Soc., xv, 157; A. W. Pollard, 'Regulation of the Book Trade', *The Library* (1916), vii, 20; see also *The Library* (1919), x, 57; F. S. Siebert, *Freedom of the Press in England. 1476-1776* (Urbana, 1952), discusses the legislation but is not always accurate in details.

8 'The Charges of our Dinner', printed in Arber, i, 57-59.

9 The introduction to *Records of the Court of the Stationers' Company 1576-1602* (London, Bib. Soc., 1930) by W. W. Greg and E. Boswell describes the constitution of the Company.

10 Richard Tottel was granted a privilege for 'all and all manner books of our temporal law' in 1553 (P.R.O., Patent roll Edward VI, pt 3, m. 29); William Seres had a similar privilege for 'certain sorts of a primer' granted in the same year (Patent Roll 7 Edward VI, pt 3, m. 35).

11 Bagford collected a number of Bynneman's title-pages. B.M. Harl. MSS., 5927.

12 The inventory (P.R.O. Statute Stable Proceedings, 34 Elizabeth, C 152/36) is partially printed in 'Bynneman's Books' by Mark Eccles, *The Library* (June 1957), xii, 81.

13 *The Discourse of the Great Cruelty of a Widow* by John God is microfilmed at the B.M. (Mic. A. 708 (8)). For Bynneman's activity in producing classical texts, see T. W. Baldwin, *William Shakespeare's Small Latine and Lesse Greeke* (Urbana, 1944, 2 vols.).

14 Christopher Barker I's account of the privileges is printed in Arber, i, 114-16.

15 The Rev. W. H. Frere in the Historical Edition of *Hymns Ancient and Modern* (London, 1909) gives an account of the Singing Psalms.

16 The outside printing house was that at Cambridge. The contract is further described on p. 59.

17 The British Museum has very few primers. The contents are those of Seres' edition of 1560.

18 The Prayer Book agreement of October 20, 1578, is recorded in Liber A of the Stationers' Company (Bib. Soc. transcript).

19 Eustace F. Bosanquet, *English Printed Almanacks and Prognostications to 1600* (London, Bib. Soc., 1917).

20 Harry H. Hoppe, 'John Wolfe, Printer and Publisher', *The Library* (1933-4), xiv, 241.

21 There are several late hornbooks complete with alphabet in the Constance Meade Collection at the University Press, Oxford. See also A. W. Tuer, *History of the Horn-Book* (London, 1897).

22 Liber A of the Stationers' Company, May 26, 1584, the Master and Wardens were to test the force and validity of the ordinances permitting search; Greg & Boswell, *op. cit.*, October 29, 1584, Wardens allowed expenses for procuring an Act of Parliament or 'any other good authority on matters tending to the commodity of the house'; same, May 7, 1586, notes expenses on the Star Chamber case; same, July 18, 1586, Christopher Barker offered £5 to the Company's counsel and a week later the other privileged printers emptied their pockets.

23 Greg & Boswell, *op. cit.*, for the searches.

24 The information on Day's privilege is found chiefly in Greg & Boswell, *op. cit.* There are one or two references in Liber A.

II

The Book Trade in
the Seventeenth Century

A T the death of Queen Elizabeth in March 1603 the privileges
once granted to John Day and William Seres were virtually
in the hands of the governing body of the Stationers'
Company, the Court of Assistants. These privileges included the
ABC and Catechism, the psalter and the primer: all the instru-
ments of basic education and private religion. After the accession
of James I the operation of these properties was transformed,
when the new King—himself an author—granted to the Company
by letters patent not only the copies above, but almanacs as well.[1]
This grant of October 1603 was crucial for the trade of printing and
publishing. The new patent differed from all preceding patents.
Superficially, it might seem only that an accomplished fact had
been legalized, or at least set upon a more realistic footing. But
what made the patent unique was that the grant was made not to one
man or to a selected partnership but to the Company as a whole.

The grant was to benefit the poor, who were thereby
guaranteed £200 a year. The purpose was laudable, and the
former partners in Day's privilege could undoubtedly well spare
such an allotment. But the royal patent itself had to be paid for—
that was usual. Then, various private persons who still participated
in the superseded privileges—John Wolfe's widow, for instance,
still had an interest in the hornbook ABC—these people had to be
bought out. The almanac patent had to be acquired, for that had
never belonged to Day or Seres. Not only had provision to be
made for these purchases, but the new patent had to be worked,
and it could not be worked without capital. Lastly, there was the
commitment to a disbursement of £200 a year.

The Court of Assistants took counsel among themselves, and it was decided that the sum, astronomical for those days, of £9,000 must be raised.[2] It was to be divided into 105 shares, scaled according to the three grades in the Company: the yeomanry or freemen, the livery and the Assistants. The scaling is instructive. The yeomen paid only £50 for their shares, which could be held between two persons. But how many yeomanry shares were available? Only 60, and there were about 400 yeomen. The livery paid twice as much, £100, and 30 liverymen out of about 75 had a chance to possess a share—just under half in that rank. So we come to the Assistants. They were to pay four times as much as the yeomen: £200 a share. But how many Assistants' shares were there? Only 15, and until the Civil War period there were never more than 15 Assistants. Thus, each one would have a slice of what promised to be a delicious cake.

It is interesting to note the wealth of these top-ranking Stationers, for few tradesmen in those days could readily have found £200 to invest. It is also interesting—and will prove significant—that each and every Assistant was vitally concerned in the new patent, whereas only half the livery could hold shares and less than 10 per cent. of the yeomanry. Lastly, the general participation of the Court is interesting because it testified to the confidence that the investment would yield more than 10 per cent., that being the normal rate of interest at the period.

These financial arrangements brought into existence what became known as the 'English Stock'. The affairs of the Company, and, therefore, of the book publishing and printing trade, henceforth revolved round the English Stock. Printing in seventeenth-century London was dominated by this Stock and its history took the course it did because of the existence of this Stock.

Only recently has the English Stock been studied. Updike followed authorities on the period when he blamed the decline in typography on 'a burdensome censorship'.[3] Like Reed, he saw State restrictions close down upon the trade after John Day's death, so that all healthy competition was crushed. These State restrictions are condemned as a 'piece of oppression which had no parallel in any other civilized country'. This was an exaggeration; but the English Stock also had no parallel in any other country, and it, rather than the Government, may well be cast as the villain when the dramatis personae is revised.

Scholars were hampered because the monumental volumes of Arber contained only a transcription in full of the registers of the Company, containing the titles entered at Stationers' Hall, with reference to a few other documents and a record of sundry payments. Not until recent years has it been possible to examine the many other surviving records, and in particular, the minutes of Court meetings. As the result of the Company's policy towards research, adopted for reasons that no doubt seemed valid at the end of the nineteenth century, it was not apparent to scholars such as R. B. McKerrow how joyfully the printers and the booksellers had welcomed restrictions on the trade, and to what degree those restrictions were the consequence of the Company's efforts during the seventeenth century to protect the new patent and to enlarge its scope.[4] These efforts were vigorous during the period held to be the Dark Ages of English printing, ages so dark by typographical standards that Updike illustrated no work from London between 1574 and 1734, with the exception of one small specimen sheet.

Whereas before October 1603 only the partners in the Day-Seres privileges had been concerned in the protection of their copies, the entire Company was now involved. Those who did not yet have Stock shares expected to obtain them. There was a fairly rapid turnover, for it was possible to sell or mortgage a share, and mortgaging was generally practised. After October 1603, therefore, it was an offence against the whole Company to pirate psalters or primers or almanacs. The case of Nathaniel Butter was typical. He was a bookseller full of enterprising ideas —he will be found taking a leading part in the history of the periodical press—and one of these ideas was to arrange for the primer to be printed for him abroad. That was in 1611. The Company expressed such horror when his misdeed was exposed that he might be thought to have murdered the Master and Wardens. He was arraigned because he had 'unjustly, undutifully, and deceitfully and deliberately, wittingly and willingly' offended against the Company's patent.[5] The only punishment that could be inflicted was forfeiture of his yeoman's share; but that was sufficient. Butter was brought to heel and never again did he offend in that respect.

Thus, the effect of the Stock was to make the Company a body more closely-knit than it had ever been before, and one disci-

7 Ye Princes ope your gates, stand ope
the euerlasting gate:
For there shall enter in thereby,
the King of glorious state.
8 Who is the King of glorious state?
the strong and mighty Lord:
The mighty Lord in battell stout,
and triall of the sword.

9 Ye Princes ope your gates, stand ope
the euerlasting gate:
For there shall enter in thereby,
the King of glorious state.
Who is the King of glorious state?
the Lord of hosts it is:
The kingdome and the royalty,
of glorious state is his.

Ad te Domine. Psal. xxv. T. S.

*David grieved at his sins, and malicious ene-
mies, most fervently prayeth for forgivenesse,
especially of such sinnes as he committed in
his youth.*

Lift my heart to thee, my God and

guide most iust: Now suffer me to take

no shame, for in thee doe I trust. 2. Let

not my foes reioice, nor make a scorne of

me: And let them not be ouerthrowne,

that put their trust in thee.

3 But shame shall them befall,
which harme them wrongfully:
Therefore thy paths & thy right waies,
vnto me Lord descrie.
4 Direct me in thy truth,
and teach me, I thee pray:
Thou art my God and Sauiour,
on thee I waite alway.

5 Thy mercies manifold,
I pray thee Lord remember:
And eke thy pitty plentifull,
for they haue beene for euer.
6 Remember not the faults,
and frailty of my youth:
Remember not how ignorant
I haue beene of thy truth.

Nor after my deserts,
let me thy mercy haue:
But of thine owne benignity,
Lord haue me in thy mind.
7 His mercy is full sweet,
his truth a perfect guide:
Therefore the Lord will sinners teach,
and such as goe aside.

8 The humble he will teach
his precepts for to keepe:
He will direct in all his waies,
the lowly and the meeke.
9 For all the waies of God,
are truth and mercy both:
To them that keepe his Testament,
the witnesse of his troth.

The second part.

10 Now for thy holy Name,
O Lord I thee intreat,
To grant me pardon for my sin,
B 3   for;

Fig. 9. A comparatively well-printed opening of the
Singing Psalms has been chosen so that the text can be
compared with the version in the Book of Common Prayer.
Page size 5½ × 3½ in.

plined with relative ease, since no man would wittingly or willingly lose not merely his investment but its steady profits. And how steady those profits were! The Singing Psalms, for instance, went through four editions in 1604, three in 1605, two in 1606, four in 1607, four again in 1609, four in 1610, six in 1612. Not a year passed without two or more editions.

There was no licensing, no 'burdensome censorship', of the Singing Psalms. On the contrary, the Government and the Church were glad that the country should be well supplied. And yet the Singing Psalms were among the most slovenly pieces of printing ever distributed from London. The paper was wretched stuff and the ink was spread as thinly as rationed butter. The separate music sorts that were always used required more than ordinary care in composition and printing—and they received less. There was no time for 'dwell'—that moment when the experienced pressman lingers to ensure that each serif has received its due allocation of ink and transferred it in sharp outline to the paper. The standards were those of the 'winkle-bag' establishment today.

The solution would have been to permit more presses. But this was not in the interest of the printers. The Stock was providing them with more work than Day or Seres had ever given since it was able to draw upon substantial capital, and they were eager to restrict this work to themselves. They did not want competitors, they did not want to see the profits spread as thinly as their ink.

Like the Singing Psalms, the primer throve, although its name was beginning to carry to the ears of Puritans of the time overtones of popery that were not wholly agreeable. The almanacs were a sounder proposition, and this little copy quickly proved to be what the Queen's Printer had called it in 1582, 'a pretty commodity to an honest man's living'.[6] But, since it was a single sheet, it was vulnerable, and pirated almanacs constantly disturbed the tranquillity of those who held English Stock.

It was natural that the Company should not confine itself to the copies granted in the patent but should enter copies in the register in the same way as the individual printer or bookseller. The policy was to buy up the tried and popular copies that came on the market, usually through a member's decease. Only a few days after the grant of the patent the Master, Wardens and Commonalty entered some collected works and religious books, including

D

the catechism of Stephen Egerton, Rector of St Anne's, Black-friars. This work went through no less than 39 editions as a Stock book. In 1612 a number of classical authors much used in grammar schools was entered to the Stock partners. By 1620 a list of Stock properties contained no less than 50 lawbooks, all the classical authors and texts in general use, all the primary educational books, works of such broad appeal as Foxe's *Martyrs*, Stow's *Chronicles*, Tusser's *Husbandry*, together with the pleasant line of thirteen books of private prayer.[7]

The rewards of the Stockholders were highly agreeable. At a later date an outsider maintained the dividend was 60 per cent, and though this may be an overestimate, even half 60 per cent would be acceptable. And had the prospects not been so sweet, the Company as a whole would have rebelled against a monopoly which controlled every best-selling line except those held by the King's Printers. In fact, there were very few protests. Edward Aldee, a printer restricted to the less profitable copies, declared of the Court that 'not an honest man sat at the Table', but he quickly retracted and apologized for behaviour he admitted to be 'turbulent'.[8]

The charge that can be sustained against the English Stock is that it took no risks. The possession of some sure-selling titles will normally encourage a publisher to venture on a work likely to appeal only to a limited audience. The Stock never ventured in this way, and prevented others from doing so by withholding the possibility of balancing accounts. Indeed, it was fortunate for English scholarship that James I's pretensions to learning were not unfounded. At least his known interest brought into print certain works that there would otherwise have been little incentive to publish. John Bill, one of the King's Printers, particularly deserves credit in this respect (see Plate IV).

In general the Stock laid a dead hand on all initiative in publishing. The stockholders and the would-be stockholders accepted a policy that guaranteed the dividend. Nor was there any incentive to raise printing or typographical standards, to experiment in any way. The restrictions of 1586 continued in force and, as far as the Company was concerned, were rigorously enforced. They included the restrictions on type, indeed on all equipment, and on apprentices. For the first forty years of the seventeenth century the number of master printers and printing houses changed

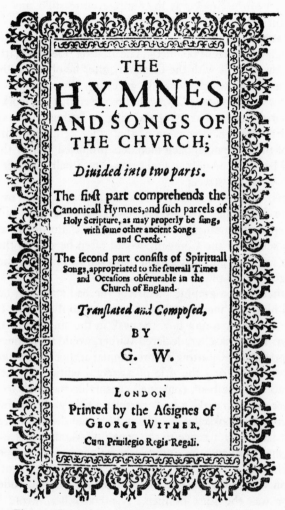

THE
HYMNES
AND SONGS OF
THE CHVRCH;

Diuided into two parts.

The first part comprehends the
Canonicall Hymnes, and such parcels of
Holy Scripture, as may properly be sung,
with some other ancient Songs
and Creeds.

The second part consists of Spirituall
Songs, appropriated to the seuerall Times
and Occasions obserueable in the
Church of England.

Translated and Composed,

BY

G. W.

LONDON
Printed by the Assignes of
GEORGE WITHER.
Cum Priuilegio Regis Regali.

Fig. 10. Page size $5\frac{1}{2} \times 3\frac{1}{2}$ in.

hardly at all. Little new blood was entering the Company, and the effect of the Stock was to cramp, even to stifle, any spirit of adventure.[9]

An attack on the Company launched in 1625 gives some information about current practices. The attacker, George Wither, the poet, was at odds with the Company after he obtained from the King a patent which not only gave him the monopoly of his *Hymns and Songs of the Church*, but required that this work should be inserted in every copy of the Singing Psalms. Naturally, the Company were having none of that: they refused point-blank. One of the more outspoken members promised Wither that they would be prepared only to find a one-legged ballad-singer to roar the songs in the streets.

Thus, Wither's attack on the Company was far from impartial; but he based his charges on general grounds and some are independently confirmed. For instance, he claimed that seditious books seized by the Company would often be sold to the profit of the searcher, and it is known that even members of the Court indulged in this practice.[10]

Wither drew a graphic picture of the bad stationer, or, as he called him, the 'mere' stationer—a man who if he came to office in the Company forgot how to speak in the singular of the first person. The bookseller, declared Wither, would take money under false pretences by putting a more popular author's name on a title-page or by altering the title of a second edition. Or he would pretend that the book contained censorable material, to make a quicker sale. To make a book popular a title would be invented, and since the bookseller would not have read the volume, his title might have no reference to the contents. Manuscripts would be published without the author's permission—this happened to Sir Thomas Browne and his *Religio Medici*, but the authorized version was worse typographically than the pirated. Indeed, the author was the least of men. The bookseller, wrote Wither, would 'fawn' upon his authors at first acquaintance and 'ring them to his hive by the promising sounds of some good entertainment'—a chink-chink of glasses, perhaps—'but as soon as they have prepared the honey to his hand, he drives the bees to seek another stall'.

Wither was less vehement against the printers and book-binders, though the latter might bind a book to last only until it

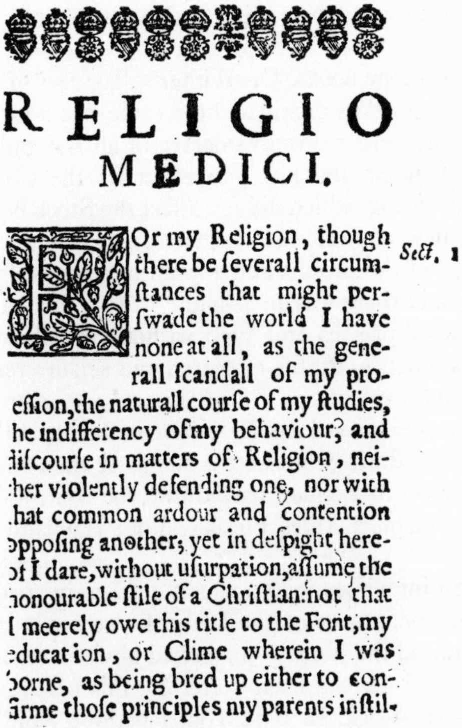

RELIGIO
MEDICI.

Or my Religion, though *Sect.* 1
there be severall circum-
stances that might per-
swade the world I have
none at all, as the gene-
rall scandall of my pro-
ession, the naturall course of my studies,
he indifferency of my behaviour, and
discourse in matters of Religion, neither violently defending one, nor with
that common ardour and contention
opposing another; yet in despight here-
of I dare, without usurpation, assume the
honourable stile of a Christian: not that
I meerely owe this title to the Font, my
education, or Clime wherein I was
borne, as being bred up either to con-
firme those principles my parents instil.

Fig. 11. The authorized version of 1643.
Page size $5\frac{3}{8} \times 3\frac{1}{2}$ in.

was sold. In his opinion, both were the slaves of the booksellers.
These craftsmen laboured for the bookseller, at the bookseller's
own prices, and the products were disposed of by the booksellers as they pleased. So the whole commonwealth, cried
Wither, was brought into bondage.[11]

The situation was not wholly dark. Wither admitted that there
were 'good' stationers, men who respected scholarship and did
not try to cheat the public. But he believed them to be rare. And
a situation such as he described was likely to arise when the booksellers were thriving and gaining more and more power within the
Company. The profitable lines of the English Stock pleased the
booksellers, whose accounts showed a rapid turnover. They did
not want the uneconomic lines which had hung so long on Bynneman's hands. The situation had changed since the sixteenth

century. Fewer and fewer printers themselves sold books; more and more often, books were printed by so-and-so for so-and-so, the latter being the bookseller. Wither's diagnosis of the extent to which the booksellers dominated the trade was not inaccurate.

In 1637 the most restrictive decree of all was published from the Star Chamber and put into effect by the Company. The system of licensing, which did not affect the Stock books but bore hardly on new copies, was tightened. The number of master printers and of the presses and apprentices they might keep was reaffirmed, and there was an absolute ban on the manufacture or importation of presses and type without permission from the Company's officials. Rights of search and seizure remained with the company.

All that was backward and restrictive in the capital's book trade was aggravated during the 1630s when more than one-fifth of the printing presses in London passed into the control of three men working in alliance: Miles Flesher, John Haviland and Robert Young.

Their first important joint action was taken in 1629, when they secured the assignment of the lawbook patent. It is not known how they raised the money—none had obvious resources. Until that year the Stock had been exercising this patent, but the trio outprinted the Stock. In 1632 Young became King's Printer in Scotland, assisted by his two colleagues. In that year they negotiated with Roger Norton a 21-year lease of the immensely profitable grammar patent that he had inherited (see Plate VI). This again interfered with the plans of the Stock, which had recently entered a number of Greek and Latin schoolbooks. To their substantial publishing empire the trio added in 1634 the lease of the patent of the King's Printer in England. This gave them the Bible and the Book of Common Prayer.[12]

The trio were able to exercise all the leases because by 1635 they controlled no fewer than nine printing presses, either by the death of their own original partners or by acquiring an interest in the printing house of a widow. The lease of the King's Printing House in London gave them at least six more, and they had others in Scotland. Never in the history of English printing—short as this was in the 1630s—had so many presses been in the hands of one controlling interest. Yet, with all this power, Flesher, Haviland and Young remained outside the governing body of the

POEMS.

By J. D.

WITH

ELEGIES

ON THE AUTHORS
DEATH.

LONDON.

Printed by *M.F.* for IOHN MARRIOT,
and are to be fold at his fhop in St *Dunftans*
Church-yard in *Fleet-ftreet.* 1633.

Fig. 12. Depth of type area 6$\frac{1}{16}$ in.
The top right-hand corner of the page,
including 's', is damaged.

Company: not one of them was an Assistant. Their achievement shows what was possible to determined men working in alliance. They had, however, exceptional gifts, Young for ruthless economics, Flesher as a skilful negotiator. They were brigands; they were locusts; and they were execrable printers without the least interest in presswork or typography.

These three men controlled the printing trade in London throughout the 1630s. It is against such a setting that the decline in English printing and typography during the seventeenth century must be viewed. Their consistent policy buttressed the effect of the English Stock, and they reinforced the low standards that passed into accepted currency when printing was freed from restrictions. Their supremacy did not mean that the printers in general acquired more power; Flesher, Haviland and Young considered only their own interests.

How they raised the considerable sums that were needed for the leases and for the Scottish patent remains a mystery; how they made money afterwards is no secret. The Archbishop of Canterbury was petitioned by Young's correctors of the press, whose salaries had been slashed. The trio were accused of employing cheap labour—unentered apprentices and foreign journeymen. In spite of their control of so many 'vendible copies', they preyed on the copies of other men: when Michael Sparkes entered *The English Gentlewoman* at Stationers' Hall, they entered *The Complete Gentlewoman*, a title that obviously would clash.[13]

Their most outrageous piracy was in 1632. The Stock had agreed on a reprint of that evergreen best-seller, Foxe's *Martyrs*. Young was one of the three printers who contracted for the work and sixteen Stockholders took up the impression. Unwisely, they paid over their money before printing was complete. To the indignation of the Company, it was then discovered that Young, far from completing his share, was engaged with Flesher and Haviland upon an impression of the abridged *Martyrs*, a brazen attempt to swamp the market with a cheaper book.[14]

Such men would not miss an opportunity to line their pockets by raising prices, an opportunity offered since they controlled the entire production of Bibles and Prayer Books, grammars and lawbooks. In addition to the usual profit, they were making £500 to £1,500 on every impression. There was not a trick they missed: cramming more on each page to give fewer workings,

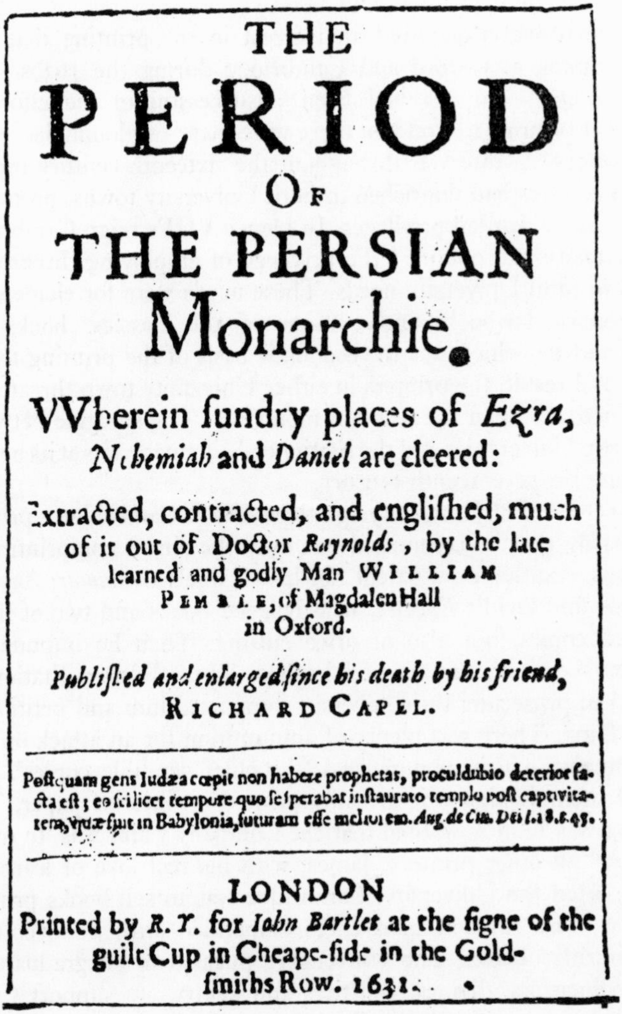

THE
PERIOD
OF
THE PERSIAN
Monarchie.

VVherein sundry places of *Ezra*,
Nehemiah and *Daniel* are cleered:

Extracted, contracted, and englished, much
of it out of Doctor *Raynolds* , by the late
learned and godly Man W I L L I A M
P E M B L E, of Magdalen Hall
in Oxford.

Published and enlarged since his death by his friend,
R I C H A R D C A P E L.

Postquam gens Iudæa cœpit non habere prophetas, proculdubio deterior facta est ; eo scilicet tempore quo se sperabat instaurato templo post captivitatem, quæ suit in Babylonia, futuram esse meliorem. *Aug de Ciu. Dei li. 3. c. 45.*

LONDON
Printed by *R. Y.* for *Iohn Bartlet* at the signe of the
guilt Cup in Cheape-side in the Gold-
smiths Row. 1631.   •

Fig. 13. Type area, including rules, 6 × 3¾ in.

advertising a fine paper edition when the paper was only less contemptible than usual, and so on.

The trio also acquired an interest in the printing that was blossoming at Oxford and Cambridge during the 1630s. The Stationers' Company had been unsuccessful in the effort to restrict printing to London: there were these two loopholes in the provinces. At intervals throughout the sixteenth century individual printers had flourished in both University towns, protected by vaguely worded privileges. In Henry VIII's reign Cambridge University had obtained the privilege of employing three printers to fulfil University needs. These needs were for elementary textbooks, lawbooks and editions of the classics, books the demand for which was the economic basis of the printing trade, and as a result, the printers in either University town threatened to encroach upon the London monopoly. The struggle between the two Universities and the Stationers' Company was at its height during the seventeenth century.

At the end of James I's reign there was at Cambridge a printer so hardy that he committed not only the sin of comprinting— that is, printing on a patent not his—Lillie's *Grammar*, Aesop's *Fables* and Ovid's *Epistles*, all privileged books and two of them Stock copies, but also of price cutting. Then he impudently embarked upon the Singing Psalms. The affronted Stationers tried to prosecute; the University supported him and petitioned the King. There was plenty of ammunition for an attack on the Company, which monopolized 'the chief vendible copies', and sold them at high prices, badly printed on inferior paper. The King was bluntly warned that the Company's aim was 'to overthrow' all other printers. James, with his real love of learning, supported the University: Cambridge was to sell books printed there. The London booksellers responded with a boycott of Cambridge books. The University appealed to all graduates— schoolmasters, divines, courtiers and gentry—to support Cambridge printing; and the Stationers saw they might reap the consequences of their failure to cultivate the friendship of men of learning.[15]

Supported by the King's interest, the University of Cambridge was able to obtain an agreement whereby the local printer might undertake Bibles and as many of the Prayer Book and the Psalms as were needed to bind with the Bibles. Further, Cambridge might print up to 3,000 each year of Lillie's *Grammar*, to be sold directly to the Stationers. This was the beginning of the so-called 'treaties of service' between Cambridge and the Company, by which the printers approved by the University worked off contracts of privileged books for London.

Oxford watched these developments. The Archbishop of Canterbury, William Laud, was an Oxford man, who longed to see established in that University a press capable of printing the ancient manuscripts that lay in the college libraries. So, in 1636 he obtained for Oxford a charter which gave that University the right to comprint all books and to have three printers, each with two presses and two apprentices. He begged the University not to endanger this charter by printing Bibles, grammars and so forth; but he begged in vain.[16]

The snag was that the printers at Oxford, like those at Cambridge, had to earn a living in the same way as the London printers. Since the University gave them no financial support, the University Presses, as they now are, did not exist. The printers had to work on what had the best sale, and to induce a printer to undertake a Greek manuscript, the Vice-Chancellor had to allow him to print almanacs. And that the Stationers were not likely to ignore.

Oxford claimed that the charter gave what was termed an 'overriding licence'. Unlike Cambridge, the older University was not ready to enter into a treaty of service. A different arrangement was concluded with the Company in 1637: the Stationers were to pay the University an annuity of £200 a year to forbear printing certain privileged books, an arrangement termed 'a covenant of forbearance'. Of the sum the Stock was to contribute £100 for the almanacs, primers and psalters, the King's Printers £80 for the Bible and the Book of Common Prayer, and Roger Norton £20 for grammar books. The University planned to allow the annuity to accumulate until learned printing could be established on a sound financial basis. It was thought that the Company would be forced to continue payment, since defection would mean that the local printers would be set to comprint.

☆

By the end of the 1630s the structure of the book trade was simple: the Stationers' Company was thriving because of the

English Stock and controlled four-fifths of the printing houses in London, the remainder being in the hands of Flesher, Haviland and Young. Printing was established at Cambridge and working to satisfy the needs of London; printing existed at Oxford but so far offered no serious competition.

The situation was wholly changed after 1640. Parliament became the effective instrument of government. In 1641 the Court of the Star Chamber was abolished and the royal prerogative went the same way; the printing trade was freed from all restrictions. There were exciting consequences as soon as printing houses could be freely stocked. The periodical press began to flourish and jobbing was a branch of ever-increasing importance. Within the Stationers' Company itself there was a revolt against monopolies.

There had been nothing like this revolt since Wolfe's, sixty years before, sixty glorious years during which not a protest had been raised against the oppressive ordinances held necessary to protect the English Stock. Wolfe had comprinted, but the new rebel, a bookseller, chose a different approach: he wrote an exposure of the evils of monopoly, *Scintilla or a Light Broken Into Dark Warehouses*. What makes this little tract still lively is not its fine writing—the bookseller, appropriately named Michael Sparkes, could not compose a sentence—but the flaming anger that blazes in each line and carries conviction.

Sparkes attacked seven patents, all of which were in the hands of Miles Flesher and Robert Young—Haviland was dead. He mentioned their names twice, but it is not clear whether he understood that they were in every case the culprits. Thus, the attack was not really against the Company but against those who might be called fellow-travellers. That Sparkes was slightly off target does not alter the facts, since the practices of Flesher and Young were also those of the Company. Sparkes marshalled damning charges: the wretched production and the ruthless extermination of all competition. Whenever he referred to a book he quoted the actual selling price, followed by the price that should have been set, and he calculated the immense profits that were being made under each monopoly.[17]

It was these revelations that upset the Stationers and forced them to take notice of Sparkes: 'all the secrets and mysteries of this profession were laid open,' they declared, 'tending much to the ruin of the English Stock'. They feared their turn would come when Sparkes hinted at his readiness to let light into other dark warehouses. *Scintilla* was addressed to Parliament, and Parliament was known to be eager to free the commonwealth from tyranny and from monopoly.

Like Wolfe, Sparkes found supporters, and within the Company he led a demand that the number of Assistants should be increased to twenty or twenty-four, which meant that not all could hold English Stock. Some new Assistants were co-opted, but it cannot have been Sparkes' intention that one was Flesher. This great negotiator was to prove invaluable to the Company once he entered the fold. Perhaps the abolition of the Star Chamber in 1641 and the death of Young in 1643 convinced Flesher that his heyday as a monopolist was over and he decided to carve a new career.

Sparke's rebellion had considerable success. During the Civil War period and the beginning of the Commonwealth, nearly all important matters were decided by committees rather than by the Court, and on those committees Sparkes and his friends often had a place. And when there was an opportunity for the Company to exercise a Bible monopoly, this was not *ipso facto* put in the hands of the English Stock. Instead, an effort was made to give it to the Company as a whole (see p. 87).[18]

The English Stock did not have an easy time during this period. Like the Book of Common Prayer, the primer was no longer popular, and in 1651 it was altogether suppressed. This was not so much because the primer smacked of popery as because the various religious sects among the Puritans did not have in prayer the same objects as Anglicans of a century before: 'a competent living' was no longer thought to be the greatest gift the Almighty could bestow.

A new service book was needed and Parliament appointed an Assembly of Divines to undertake the momentous task. Very soon the Company was petitioning the Divines for 'all such things for public use as hereafter shall pass the Assembly'. The form of public service worked out by the Divines was called *The Directory for Public Worship* and, in their simplicity, the Divines gave it to four stationers, including a typefounder, Alexander Fifield, of whom not one was prominent in the Company. Flesher's talent quickly found employment and after negotiation

Of the Solemnization of Marriage. 63

ried wife, and doe, in the preſence of God, and before this Congregation, promiſe and covenant to be a loving and faithfull husband unto thee, untill God ſhall ſeparate us by death.

Then the woman ſhall take the man by his right hand, and ſay theſe words,

I N. *doe take thee* N. *to be my maried husband, and I doe, in the preſence of God, and before this Congregation, promiſe and covenant to be a loving, faithfull, and obedient wife unto thee, untill God ſhall ſeparate us by death.*

Then, without any further Ceremony, the Miniſter ſhall, in the face of the Congregation, pronounce them to be husband and wife, according to Gods Ordinance; and ſo, conclude the action with Prayer to this effect,

That

Fig. 14. *The Directory for the Public Worship of God*, first edition 1644, was printed for Evan Tyler, Alexander Fifield, Ralph Smith and John Field, the last named being probably the printer. Page size $7\frac{1}{2} \times 5\frac{1}{2}$ in.

the four yielded the *Directory* to the English Stock.[19] The fine
first edition of 1644, one of the most attractive books printed in
the mid-century, was succeeded by the usual careless, cramped
and ill-executed production that was characteristic of Stock books.

The Singing Psalms were also threatened. They were not
discredited like the primer—on the contrary, Parliament commanded that all who could read should have a psalmbook from
which to sing tunefully. But it was natural that Puritan scholars
should wish to try their hand at translating into metre the Psalms
of David. Flesher was invoked to conduct negotiations with a
series of these individualists. They all came in, though there was
one uneasy Court day, when two translators, having promised to
attend, failed to put in an appearance. But they succumbed, and
after 'great debate'—that familiar phrase in Court reports—an
agreement was reached.

Though the almanacs were not challenged by Parliament or
Divines, the Stock was much harassed by pirates after all could
print freely. No Stockholder welcomed the lifting of restrictions.
As early as 1643 the Company was petitioning for an Act to
suppress the hawkers employed by the periodical publishers. The
booksellers were severely hit by the economic circumstances of
civil war: 'the deadness of the time' appeared often as an excuse
for unpaid debts. The printers were becoming more important in
the Company than they had been since the early years of Elizabeth's reign. This led to no improvement in standards of typography or presswork.

Frames, vignettes and house blocks had disappeared from title
pages just before the Civil War, but fleurons of inferior design and
poor condition were much used. It is possible, however, to
exaggerate the poor quality of the printing: this was an age of
popular and cheap books and tracts, and such work tends to be
poorly produced at any period. The founders were busy cutting
smaller type sizes, for books had now to be carried in the pocket.[20]
Periodicals and jobbing created new demands for men and equipment. Founding, composing, printing and binding had to be done
at high speed, for there was more work than the country's
printing houses could handle. But the Company did not welcome
the uncontrolled expansion of the trade.

Meanwhile, Parliament was discovering the wisdom successive
kings had shown in their control of the printing press: much of

Justice upon the Armie

REMONSTRANCE.

OR

A rebuke of that evill spirit that leads them
in their Counsels and Actions.

With

*A Discovery of the contrariety and enmity in
their waies, to the good spirit and
minde of God.*

Dedicated

To the Generall, and the Councel of War.

By William Sedgwick.

---

*But they shall proceed no further, for their
folly shall be manifest to all men.* 2 Tim. 3. 9.

LONDON,
Printed for *Henry Hils,* and are to be sold at his house
over against S. *Thomases* Hospitall in *Southwark,* and at
the Black *Spread-Eagle* at the West end of *Pauls,*
neare *Ludgate.* M. DC. XLIX.

Fig. 15. Type area, including borders, $6\frac{11}{16} \times 4\frac{5}{8}$ in.

the work being produced during the Civil War period was too controversial or too outspoken to please those newly come to power. The Stationers' Company was required to prevent 'disorderly' printing, but the Company itself was torn by the civil war Sparkes had begun and its authority had to be reinforced by Parliament before it could regain control of the trade. Restrictions were reimposed on printing by an Act of 1649 and joyfully the Company's searchers were instructed to resume their labours. A second Act was passed in 1652, many Stationers having attended at Westminster when the bill was passing in order to 'improve their several interests to promote it'.[21]

There was no attempt by Parliament to prune the number of master printers, which had approximately doubled since 1637, and certain places other than London had their right to a printing house acknowledged. These were victories for the periodical publishers, who continued to vex and defy the Company. Petitions were prepared at Stationers' Hall for further legislation and when in 1655 Cromwell suppressed all periodical publishing with the exception of two official newspapers, a grave threat to the supremacy of the Court was removed. On the other hand, Cromwell actively encouraged the existence of another threat; John Field and Henry Hills, neither of whom cared a straw for the Company's interests, were appointed Printers to his Highness.

No regulations could halt the decline of the English Stock and during the decade before the Restoration the dividend was rarely more than 6 per cent, supplemented by a distribution of Stock books.[18] By 1660 the printers within the Company were so strong that they planned to break away and form their own organization. It was as well they did not do so: the troubles of the trade were by no means at an end. The return of Charles II in 1660 did not usher in a period of prosperity such as the Stock had enjoyed in the reign of Charles I.

At first the King seemed favourable towards the Company—at least, the protection of copyright in general and almanacs in particular was one of his first actions. But in 1662, two years later, a new Act to regulate printing was promulgated, one by no means so welcome in all respects to the Company as its predecessors. The number of master printers, now grown to 59, was to wither until it reached 20. They might have only two presses and two apprentices each though, as before, past officials of the Company

E

might have three. All books were to be licensed, and the licence was now printed facing the title page. So far, there was little change. The injury to the Company lay in a new clause: Stationers' Hall was no longer to be responsible for search and seizure. This power was to rest with the Secretary of State, who in 1663 appointed Sir Roger L'Estrange Surveyor of the Press.

After this the Company began to feel the whip. Since L'Estrange had been granted a monopoly of news publications, he had a lively interest in the suppression of unlicensed printing. He did not believe that the Company was sincere in its professed willingness to suppress unlicensed periodicals, and he was justified in this belief, for as always the Company's chief interest was the protection of copyright. L'Estrange brought more than twenty printers to trial. The Stationers charged him with the intention of making them slaves, but they were helpless since L'Estrange had the ear of the Government and they were much weakened by the ravages of the Plague in 1665 and the Great Fire in 1666.

L'Estrange himself calculated that over eighty of the printing trade were carried off by the deadly infection, and the number of master printers in the capital was abruptly reduced to twenty-eight. In the Plague the Stationers lost lives, in the Fire they lost stocks. The effect was catastrophic. The surviving twenty-eight were stripped of their presses, type and paper as well as their premises, the booksellers lost their wares and their shops. Only the corporate efforts of the Company enabled the trade slowly to recover. There was some consolation in that the prices of what books did survive were much enhanced, and the demand from Londoners who had lost libraries, and schools that had lost text-books, offered a chance of revival.

These disasters occurred at a time when Oxford University had begun to print on some scale. The covenants of forbearance had been resumed in 1656 and reaffirmed after the Restoration. But the Vice-Chancellor, Doctor Fell of 'I do not like thee, Doctor Fell', intended to realize Laud's ambition of a learned press. The Sheldonian Theatre was equipped as a printing house and after 1669 a series of well executed books in specially procured type faces appeared to compete with the London trade.[16]

In London standards of typography and presswork showed little improvement. The career of the title page was typical.

AN

EXPOSITION

OF THE

Thirty=nine Articles

OF THE

CHURCH of ENGLAND.

Written by

GILBERT Bishop of *SARUM.*

LONDON:

Printed by *R. Roberts*, for R i. C H I S W E L L, at the *Rose and Crown* in St. *Paul's* Church-Yard. M D C X C I X.

Fig. 16. Type area, including rules, $10\frac{3}{8} \times 5$ in.

Ornament, whole or battered, had been generally abandoned and the vogue was for red and black, a simplicity which required good letter and careful presswork. Printers had learned little since Flesher's heyday of the organization of white space, and when the title was short the result was likely to be awkward. Oxford solved the problem neatly by the use of engraved representations of the Theatre or some other feature of academic printing.

Fell discovered that it was economically impossible to confine Oxford to unprivileged books: the profits of the Bible and the Book of Common Prayer, of the Singing Psalms and the grammar were necessary to sustain learned printing. When the covenant with the Stationers expired in 1672 he declined to renew it. This was a blow the Londoners were ill equipped to meet. Both the King's Printers and Roger Norton, still alive and still the grammar patentee, had lost everything in the Fire and had since found that their market was being invaded by books printed abroad. The Stationers feared—rightly—that Oxford would comprint the Singing Psalms to bind with the Bibles. A long struggle ensued, which may be described later since it principally revolved round the Bible patent (see p. 89).

Comprinting was not the only challenge Fell presented to the Company: there was the standard of production he maintained in Oxford books. The London printer who most nearly had at heart the well-being of the trade, Joseph Moxon, author of the *Mechanick Exercises*, dedicated his book to Fell as a tribute to the latter's 'ardent affection to promote typography'—using that word to mean printing in general. But the Stationers could not be expected to acclaim books that in format were likely to appeal to the new society springing up about the royal Court. Fell was consciously intent to raise the level of English printing. He had observed how the reputation of the Dutch had risen since they practised good printing and he knew of the example set by the royal printing house of Louis XIV. He hoped that Oxford would perform the same service to his own country. A friend wrote that he wished Oxford 'whiter paper and blacker ink than commonly we have in England', and Fell chose his materials as carefully as he chose his titles. Once or twice the learned press managed to produce a best-seller, such as *The Ladies' Calling*—needless to say, the Stationers promptly comprinted.

As well as the hostility of L'Estrange and the competition of

Oxford, the Company faced another threat from an unexpected quarter: after the Restoration the status of the author slowly began to improve. This was partly due to a change in the public's taste for books. Theatres that had been closed since 1642 re-opened and became immensely popular after they had received royal patronage. Actors and actresses became as celebrated as television stars today, and playwrights and poets were idolized. This was the age of Dryden, Wycherley, Congreve, Davenant, Otway and many more, who satisfied the public's thirst for enter-tainment and light reading matter. Sermons, paradoxically, were hardly less popular.

The gentlemen who began to meet in coffee-houses met also in bookshops where the witty, sophisticated writing that they pre-ferred was selected amid lively discussion. The 'mere stationer' of Wither's day had to change his habits if he wished to attract customers. The demand for light reading matter was intensified by L'Estrange's control of the periodical press, which lasted until the last decade of the century.

This encouragement and the opportunity for full-time employ-ment, though often of hack writers, had many repercussions. New translations of the classics were demanded, new school textbooks were planned. Lillie's famous grammar, the basis of English education for two centuries, was superseded, the schoolbooks upon which the English had so long depended were out of fashion. The Singing Psalms survived, but not without serious competi-tion which the Company failed to buy in as it had bought in competitors of the pre-Restoration period. The variety of titles that had adorned the English Stock ceased to sell, and by the beginning of the eighteenth century the dividend was almost wholly derived from the Singing Psalms and the almanacs. As the need to protect Stock copyrights vanished, and as the Com-pany, withheld from search and seizure, ceased to be able effect-ively to protect any copyright, so the Company declined and its interests no longer bound the printing trade into a single body, co-operating for a common end.

The decay of the Company was sharply manifest after 1695, when all restrictions on printing were removed. The register at Stationers' Hall was no longer used to protect copies. During the whole twelve months of 1701, a typical year, only three titles were entered. This indifference did not mean that a solution to the problem of protection had been found: far from it. But it was now the booksellers, not the Company, who combined to petition Parliament for legislation. And it was the booksellers who combined, not the printers. It was the booksellers who were buyers of manuscripts and owners of copyright. The publisher of modern times was beginning to emerge.

The petitions were successful in 1709 when the Copyright Act of Queen Anne was passed. For the first time authors were granted statutory rights in their work. New books were protected for fourteen years, to be extended for a further fourteen if the author lived. Piracy was to be fined: half to the Government, half to the informer—nothing to the Stationers' Company. There was no mention of numbers of apprentices, no priority given to past Masters and Wardens. The day when the Court of Assistants sitting in Stationers' Hall had ruled the printing trade was gone for ever.

The positive elements in the 1709 Act were partly the result of the changed status of authors, and it was their new importance that had assisted to end the system of monopolies which strangled the trade during the seventeenth century. The omissions in the Act, the failure to acknowledge the Company, were partly the result of the increase in the number of periodical and jobbing printers.

But there was one patent that survived: the patent of the King's or Queen's Printers, the patent that included the Bible, the greatest of all the patents.

NOTES

1 The patent is printed in Arber, iii, 42-4.

2 William Jackson, *Records of the Court of the Stationers' Company*, 1602-40 (London, Bib. Soc., 1957). The introduction gives an excellent account of the setting up of the English Stock. See also Cyprian Blagden, 'The English Stock of the Stationers' Company in the time of the Stuarts', *The Library* (1957), xii, 167, which includes an account of the earlier period.

3 D. B. Updike, *Printing Types, their History, Forms and Use* (Oxford, 1937, 2 vols.), ii, 93. A bibliography on this point is given in the footnote.

4 R. M. McKerrow, Chapter xxiii in *Shakespeare's England* (Oxford, 1916).

5 Jackson, *op. cit.* (Letterbook), October 26, 1611.

6 Christopher Barker's report of December 1582, printed in Arber, i, 114.

7 Arber, iii, under November 28, 1603, September 21, 1612, and March 5, 1620.

8 Jackson, *op. cit.*, under June 30, 1623.

9 Lists of printing houses in 1634 and 1635, taken from the State Papers Domestic, Chas I, are printed in Arber, iii, 700-4.

10 Records of the Court 1641-55 (Bib. Soc. photostats).

11 Wither's attack, *Scholars' Purgatory, discovered in the Stationers' Commonwealth, described in a Discourse Apologetical*, is partly printed in Arber, iv, 14-20.

12 Jackson, *op. cit.*, contains a reference to the lawbook patent in the introduction, and in the records are several references to the activities of Young as King's Printer in Scotland. An account of the lease of the grammar patent (i.e. the patent of King's Printer in Hebrew, Latin and Greek) is recited in P.R.O. Chancery records, 2 Chas I, F.3.60. The details of the lease of the King's Printer's patent (England) are recited in State Papers Domestic, 1644, 16/503/part 2.

13 Sparkes entered Brathwait's *English Gentlewoman* on April 20, 1631. See Arber, iv, 251, for these entries.

14 Jackson, *op. cit.*, under August 1, 1631, and March 1, 1631/2.

15 S. C. Roberts, *The Cambridge University Press 1521-1921* (Cambridge, 1921).

16 John Johnson and Strickland Gibson, *Print and Privilege at Oxford to the year 1700* (Oxford, 1946). See Jackson, *op. cit.*, under February 13, April 3 and April 27, 1637, for Young's participation in

the agreement with Oxford. As lessees of the grammar patent, the trio were involved in the treaty of service with Cambridge.

17 *Scintilla* is printed in Arber, iv, 35-8.

18 Cyprian Blagden, 'The Stationers' Company in the Civil War Period', *The Library* (1958), xiii, 1.

19 These negotiations and those for the Psalms are found in the records of the Court 1641-55 of which the Bibliographical Society have photostats.

20 The most obvious instance is the Company's instruction to Nicholls, the typefounder, to cut type for their small Bibles (24mos), see the transcript, *op. cit.*, under March 3, 1645.

21 The Stationers' efforts are recorded in the transcript, *op. cit.* See particularly, the entries under November 23 and December 28, 1652.

22 F. S. Siebert, *Freedom of the Press in England 1476-1776* (Urbana, 1952).

III

The Bible Patent

IF A current edition of the Authorized Version of the Bible is examined one of three imprints will be found: the King's or Queen's Printers, or either of the University Presses at Oxford and Cambridge. No other publishing house in England may issue a complete text of the Authorized Version. The same rule applies to the Book of Common Prayer.

The Bible and the Book of Common Prayer are all that remain of the once numerous properties that belonged to the royal printers. The heyday of the royal patent was in the eighteenth century, when, in addition to the Bible and the Book of Common Prayer, the King's or Queen's Printers issued Statutes, Proclamations, Injunctions and Acts of Parliament, and were also, probably by virtue of the patent, Printers to the House of Lords. At this period the competition in Bible printing from the Universities was insignificant. But both Universities possessed charters that gave them an overriding licence to print all books, including those that came within the patent of the royal printers.

The patent of the royal printers only slowly developed as an exclusive right to various properties. Under Henry VII, the first known King's Printer, William Faques, was a purveyor, similar to Royal Warrant holders today. He was given proclamations and statute books to print, but granted no rights in them.[1] Faques' successor, Richard Pynson, was printer to Henry VIII, that royal author, and so Pynson printed the royal book, the *Assertion of the Seven Sacraments* (1521), which won Henry his title of Defender of the Faith. In the time of Pynson's successor, Thomas Berthelet, injunctions were required to regulate the new national Church.[2] It was not until the time of Christopher Barker in 1577 that all these properties, together with Bibles,

Testaments and the Book of Common Prayer, were formally included in a patent giving exclusive rights.

For nearly three centuries after 1577 the patent was unchanged in respect of the properties that could be printed under it, but in the course of the nineteenth century the items that related to the Government were taken away from the then Queen's Printers. This was not a disaster for them: the Stationery Office had not the equipment to print these items and, not for the first time in the patent's history, the printing was left in the hands of those who were so equipped. And secondly, the Bible and the Book of Common Prayer were always the most valuable elements in the patent.

The present account of the royal patent is confined to the Bible—the most interesting of the elements because it roused the fiercest competition. To many people in this country the Bible is a sacred book, perhaps even the inspired word of God, and that fact is relevant; but to its publishers the Bible is a book with certain physical features that make it different from all other books. First: the Authorized Version contains 774,746 words. Compositors and pressmen will quickly work out what that means in terms of ens, in paper orders and machining time. Secondly: there exists a considerable and a constant demand for the Bible. Thirdly: the Bible must be produced without a single misprint. And fourthly: the Bible is required in the whole range of sizes, from folio to the smallest.

One or two of these conditions may apply to other books, such as dictionaries and encyclopaedias; but no other book combines all four.

This combination of unusual features has always attracted to Bible printing the most shrewd businessmen in the trade. Bible printing is highly specialized, and in the past it was often possible for the patentees to take advantage of the inexperience of competitors. Since the beginning of the nineteenth century, however, there has been intense competition, and Oxford has emerged as the leading Bible house. Success brings its own problems. At a time when Oxford printed at least a dozen regular editions, these were never off the press, and the same happy state existed for a long period when Cambridge printed the Bible in Afrikaans. Such a situation creates serious difficulties, as anyone associated with a printing house will know. Among other gifts, a Bible printer needs a talent for organization and a keen analytical mind. When these were not possessed the results were disastrous.

The first printer of the English Bible in this country, Richard Grafton, had these gifts. He began his career in this field as the publisher of the so-called 'Matthew' Bible, which was printed abroad in 1537 since there did not exist in this country the typographical equipment for a work such as Thomas Cromwell,

❡ The fyrſt Chapter.
❡ The voyce of the Churche.

Fig.17. Block size 2 × 2¾ in.

Henry VIII's chief adviser, and Thomas Cranmer, the Archbishop of Canterbury, wished to supply. The Matthew Bible was a combination of William Tyndale's Pentateuch (the first five books of the Old Testament) and his New Testament, the remainder of the Old Testament being in Coverdale's translation. The text was annotated by a theologian (John Rogers) who used the pseudonym of Thomas Matthew.

These notes presented problems of setting and, in addition, the Matthew Bible was lavishly illustrated. Some of the blocks are most lively—Cain slays Abel with remarkable vigour. The Song or Ballad of Solomon, here illustrated, was printed throughout in red and black, for the first—and only—time in the history of the English Bible.

Grafton noted his expenses: the impression of 1,500 cost him

£500 (today, nearer £5,000). Actually, this figure was to prove low for Bible production in that century, but Grafton, of course, did not consider it low. He asked Cromwell to give him protection against pirates, and also to provide a market by instructing every curate to buy one copy and every monastery six.[3] His Bible being in folio size, Grafton was dependent upon orders from parishes and monasteries, and even with help he estimated that the impression would take three years to sell—three years before he saw a return upon what was for him a large investment.

Thus, at the beginning of Bible publishing in this country, it was seen that the publisher would need protection and encouragement from the authorities. Grafton also understood one of the chief difficulties of Bible printing: 'Look,' he enjoined Cromwell 'how many sentences are in the Bible—even so many faults and errors shall be made therein.' In this respect his difficulties were enhanced since he was employing Dutch compositors.

Cromwell acceded to Grafton's wishes, and an injunction, printed by the then King's Printer, Berthelet, ordered all parishes to be provided with a folio volume chained in the church. And when Cromwell planned the Great Bible, based on a revised translation by Coverdale, he employed the experienced Grafton and his associate Edward Whitchurch, first as the publishers and finally also as the printers.

The first edition of the Great Bible was printed in France. Unfortunately, before the edition was complete officers of the French Inquisition descended on the printing house and seized the sheets. Grafton had had the forethought to send some copies into safe keeping and, with the resource typical of Bible printers, he managed to trace some sheets that had been sold to a haberdasher for wrapping paper. So, a few copies were published as planned in April 1539.

The fine wood-block on the title page is sometimes ascribed to Holbein. It gave glory where, in Cromwell's opinion, glory was due: at the top, Henry VIII is distributing the Word of God to the spiritual and temporal lords; beneath his throne, Cranmer and Cromwell, in their turn, are handing it to the clergy and the laity. The circular armorial device below Cromwell, the figure on the right-hand side, had hastily to be cut out when he fell from power in July 1540, and in subsequent editions there is at this place a clumsily cut hole in the block.

There were seven editions of the Great Bible—'great' because
it was specifically 'of the largest volume', suitable to be placed in
churches for all to study. The words 'appointed to be read in the
churches' pleased Grafton and Whitchurch since they were the
sole publishers, and the venture had been financed by their
enterprise. They found other work in the officially compiled
primer and in the breviary of Salisbury Use, a service book
necessary until the Book of Common Prayer was devised.

Thus, when Henry VIII died in 1547 and his son's Government
wished to advance the Reformation, Grafton and Whitchurch
were entrenched as Bible and service-book printers. Berthelet,
the King's Printer, was a diminished figure, and he was ejected
from the patent, which was given to Grafton. The grant still did
not include Bibles or service books: in theory, the printing of
these works was left free for all, but in practice they remained
the monopoly of Grafton and Whitchurch. It was they who
printed the two versions of the Book of Common Prayer that
appeared during Edward's short reign. Grafton, in his turn, was
ejected from the patent when Mary came to the throne, since he
had misguidedly printed the Proclamation of Lady Jane Grey as
Queen. There were no English Bibles or Books of Common
Prayer licensed during Mary's reign. Her printer, John Cawood,
survived the accession of Elizabeth, but was joined in the patent
by Richard Jugge.[4]

Jugge was the first Bible printer who failed. He secured the
printing of the translation known as the Bishops' Bible, of which
the first edition appeared in 1568. In the year of the second
edition, 1572, Cawood died. The patent remained with the
longest liver, but Jugge now discovered, as later holders would
discover, that to exercise the royal patent alone was a heavy undertaking. With all the other work that flowed into his printing
house from the patent, he found difficulty in organizing the
production of Bibles. An octavo Testament took him two years
to complete, and whereas Grafton and Whitchurch had issued
seven folio Bibles in three years, Jugge managed only two in the
same period.

This rate of production was unsatisfactory to the Government
and to the Church, who wished to see a copy of the new translation available in every church. Jugge was not printing with
sufficient speed. Official pressure was put on him to share his

Bible printing with other Stationers if he could not work it alone. This was in 1575, when Jugge was Master of the Company. He took the suggestion badly: it was an affront to his dignity. After 'long hearing and debating of grievances', he was officially instructed to limit himself to the quarto Bible and to the Testament in sixteenmo. All other sizes might be printed by the Stationers. Jugge protested bitterly: he considered he was at least entitled to the quarto Testament, and the advantage of printing books in the same size is obvious. But the Stationers would not agree that he should have the monopoly of the size for which there was a rich and relatively unexplored market. Jugge yielded.[5]

He was further embarrassed by the tactics of a shrewd outsider. Christopher Barker, a wealthy draper with powerful friends, became interested in the printing trade. He obtained a privilege for the Calvinist translation of the Bible in English, already printed abroad, but not in this country. The Geneva version was different from the Bishops' Bible, and not Jugge's 'copy' at all. Neither Jugge nor the Stationers relished Barker's success. Hurriedly, ten Stationers formed a Bible partnership, and then, actually on the same day, they and Jugge met Barker, to assert their rights in the Bishops' Bible.

An ambitious campaign was opened to outprint the Genevan version. In 1575, still the same year, five Stationers, of whom William Norton was one, set their imprint on a Bible. They had the start of Barker, whose first edition did not appear until the following year. But the grand design collapsed in 1577: in that year Jugge died, and the various agreements became void. Barker was Jugge's energetic successor as royal patentee, and his grant specifically included Bibles and Testaments 'whatsoever', as well as the Book of Common Prayer.[6]

Barker's first Genevan Bible of 1576 is one of the finest pieces of English printing in the sixteenth century. The typography is not original, being faithfully based on an excellent model, the original English edition printed in Geneva, but the presswork is far above average, and care and thought have been exercised at every point. The paper is excellent, though thin. Barker followed the example of Geneva in the use of roman type—all other printers of the Bible in English had preferred blackletter.

The short time for which the Bishops' Bible and the Geneva Bible had been shared must have been of value to Barker, for it

Fig. 18. The engraved frontispiece of the Bishops' Bible, printed by Christopher Barker I, 1584.
Plate size 10 × 5¾ in.

gave him a chance to accumulate both equipment and experience
so that by the time he took over the royal patent he was fully
competent to exercise it. Considering that he came to the printing
trade late in life he showed extraordinary judgment and understanding. There is no more penetrating analysis written by a
publisher than his official report on the privileges, made in 1582.[7]
For instance, he divined what was then scarcely apparent: that the
control of the trade would pass into the hands of the booksellers.
In 1582 the only real indication of this trend was that the grammar
patent was held by at least four booksellers, one of whom,
William Norton, was hardly less capable than Barker himself.
What Barker had to say of his own patent, therefore, deserves
attention. His principal point was the cost of undertaking the
Bible. He recalled how Jugge had been unable to print. He described his own editions of the Geneva Bible as a 'desperate
adventure', costing him £3,000 over eighteen months, during
which period his finances had been to the last degree precarious.
The costs had plainly risen since Grafton's time, though we must
allow for a tendency to exaggerate. Barker's own son was to
demonstrate the truth of his father's statements. Bible printing
could not be successfully undertaken except by a man with great
financial resources, and these liquid enough for him to make a
heavy investment and to wait for slow returns.

Barker was preparing this report as a counter to John Wolfe's
attack upon the privileges (see p. 38), and, understandably, there
was reserve about profits. Indeed, Barker was pessimistic when
he wrote on the other elements in the patent. Testaments were
priced so low that costs were scarcely recovered—he did not
mention that it was convenient to work them with Bibles of the
same size. As to Proclamations, they were demanded at short
notice and unpredictable intervals, so that the ordinary routine of
the printing house had to be unprofitably disturbed to work them
off. Obviously, a small 'copy' like Proclamations, often a single
sheet, was awkwardly associated with the huge mass of the Bible;
but Barker did not mention that he was paid for Government
printing.

It was, however, such careful omissions that showed Barker's
business acumen, and enabled him to be one of the most successful patentees. No criticism was made during his tenure. As to
Bibles, he kept the country supplied with accurate texts, his

presswork was admirable, and the typography agreeable. No complaints were made of his prices, and he died in 1599, wealthy and respected.

Before his death the patent had already been secured for his son Robert. This one lacked the foresight of the father; but he was thoroughly trained and for some years printed in association with two of his father's friends, whose experience must have been valuable. For a time all went well. Robert Barker was highly regarded by his fellow Stationers, and in both 1605 and 1606, as a comparatively young man, he was Master of the Company.

He was by no means a fool; he was up to all the usual dodges. In 1606 he agreed to pay £400 to the English Stock for the octavo size of the Bishops' Bible, a leftover from the partnership in Jugge's time. He produced £100 in cash and lent the Company £50 at 10 per cent.[8] The Bishops' Bible, which was not annotated, was never popular: both Barkers, father and son, concentrated on the Geneva version, and Robert may have welcomed the project of the Authorized Version. The new King, James I, urgently pressed for this new translation, to be diligently compared with those preceding, but based on the original tongues. By 1609 the labours of the translators were ready to be welded into a single manuscript.

At this stage Barker's expenses began, for he was responsible for the payment of the collators and revisers.[9] The bill came to nearly £1,000—it would approach five figures today—and the printing and production trebled this sum. 'I do yet groan under the burden of this book', Barker wrote, when he was sending out some proofs. He was a rich man, but his capital was invested in land, and he appears to have met the burden by borrowing from William Norton's son, Bonham Norton, and, possibly, from another bookseller, John Bill. Bonham Norton may even have been responsible for part of the printing, which was shared between two offices, their products possibly distinguished as the great He Bible and the great She Bible (from an error in *Ruth*, iii, 15).

The printing was an exceptional undertaking, for not only were blackletter folios required, but other sizes in roman type. In 1613 Barker even produced a blackletter folio with fewer workings for those churches that could not afford the first edition. There was a handsome engraved title-page (see Plate VI) and plentiful

F

ornament, though the typography was again based on sixteenth-century models. The difficulties experienced in printing are reflected in the innumerable variations of collation in the sheets.

Although the Authorized Version printed by Robert Barker cannot compare with magnificent folio Bibles published abroad, it was a most remarkable and a highly creditable achievement when the range of sizes is considered. No Bible printer in this country has been required to emulate Robert Barker, for the Authorized Version is still appointed to be read in the churches, and blackletter editions are no longer required.

☆

A wiser man, such as Christopher Barker had been, would have thought carefully before engaging himself to a Norton. After 1611 begins the first of the bitter struggles that have centred on the Bible patent. Bonham Norton was determined to obtain it for himself and he saw that Barker was giving him an opportunity. Great intimacy developed between the families. The two men were closely associated in the Company and Barker was willing that his son, Christopher II, should marry Norton's daughter. Nor was this all. Barker was so embarrassed financially that he agreed to assign the patent to Norton and Bill for a year, and put his son, who would inherit the patent, into the royal printing house so that he could be guided by Norton and Bill as Robert Barker had once been guided by his father's friends.

Now Barker's troubles began. At the end of the year Norton refused to yield the patent, declaring that the assignment had been for life. He had even prevailed on Christopher II to take sides against his own father, and Barker was forced to resort to law. Not until 1620 was he able to regain the patent. And henceforth it was to be shared with John Bill, who was held to have purchased his half-share in good faith.

Norton was not content. He was a man bent on securing further power, a man of infinite resource in the pursuit of his ends, and ruthless in his manipulation of men. He was determined to control this lucrative patent, which included the right to the Authorized Version for which so great a demand existed. And the patent had then the attraction that the King's Printers were not restricted to two or three presses. Every consideration incited Norton to eject Barker, and this was soon done, on the ground that Barker had not paid the price—truly fantastic—of £11,000 which Norton claimed for his share. Poor Barker did not have time to complete an edition of the Welsh Bible upon which he had conscientiously embarked, before he once again lost the patent and the names in the imprint reverted to those of Norton and Bill.

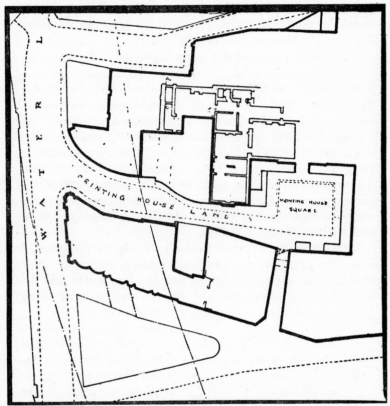

Fig. 19. Printing House Lane and Square, formerly the site of the King's Printing House, are now part of the office of *The Times*.

It was at this juncture that Norton decided to move the royal printing house, hitherto in Barker's leasehold property in Aldersgate, on the site of the present GPO. Norton and Bill settled on Hunsdon House in Blackfriars as a suitable office. It was on the present site of the Office of *The Times*. Printing House Square itself takes its name from their printing house, and the royal printing house remained there for 150 years or more, when

John Walter I, the founder of *The Times*, bought the vacant site.[10]

The ground plan of Printing House Square has changed little and visitors still walk up Printing House Lane as Norton and Bill once did. The first buildings on the left-hand side belonged to the playhouse with which Shakespeare was connected. The lane passed through an ancient gateway and into the courtyard or square—a site of great antiquity, once the inner cloister of the Priory of the Dominican or Black Friars.

The range on the east side of the courtyard, which faces the mouth of the lane, was set aside for the printing house, and elsewhere Norton and Bill arranged their own dwelling-houses. On this east side there were on the ground-floor a warehouse, a counting-house and a kitchen, and above was a gallery, one hundred feet long, used by both compositors and pressmen. The site of this gallery is now editorial offices. Two closets adjoining the gallery housed the type store and the correctors of the press. The overseer's office was probably on the opposite side of the courtyard, and by the gateway was another room where the sheets were gathered—binding was not done on the premises but in association with the booksellers.

Barker's struggle to regain Norton's share of the patent lasted nine years during which period he was vexed by every conceivable obstacle Norton could devise. At last, in 1629, Barker paid the sum demanded—now reduced to £8,000—and entered Printing House Square as one of His Majesty's Printers.

mat. 5.33. " 8 Remember the Sabbath day, to keepe it holy.
Chap.   9 * Sixe dayes shalt thou labour, and doe all
23.12.   thy worke:
ezek.20   10 But the seuenth day is the Sabbath of § LORD
22.luke   thy God: in it thou shalt not doe any worke, thou
  nor thy son, nor thy daughter, thy man-seruant, nor
  thy maid-seruant, nor thy cattle, nor thy stranger
  that is within thy gates:
*Gen.2.2.   11 For*in fix dayes the LORD made heauen and
  earth, the sea and all that in them is, and rested the
  seuenth day, wherefore the LORD blessed the Sabbath day, and hallowed it.
* Deut.5.   12 ¶ * Honour thy father and thy mother, that
16.mat.   thy dayes may bee long vpon the land which the
15.4   LORD thy God giueth thee.
ephe 6.2.   13 * Thou shalt not kill.
* Matth.   14 Thou shalt commit adultery.
5.21.   15 Thou shalt not steale.
  16 Thou shalt not beare false witnesse against
  thy neighbour
* Rom.   17 * Thou shalt not couet thy nighbours house,
7.7.   thou shalt not couet thy neighbours wife, nor his
  man-seruant, nor his maid-seruant, nor his oxe, nor
  his asse, nor any thing that is thy neighbours.

Fig. 20. Exodus xx, see verse 14.
Column width, 12 picas.

But Norton refused to acknowledge defeat. He publicly vilified Barker in disgraceful terms, he incited his relations to interrupt the printing—even to steal the composing irons—and in the end it seems probable that he suborned the workmen to allow a blasphemous misprint to pass. So the 'Wicked' Bible appeared in 1631, with 'not' omitted from the Seventh Commandment.

To realize how distressing

it was for the injunction to appear as 'Thou shalt commit adultery', it is necessary to imagine this page being read by someone earnest but relatively uneducated, whose Bible was perhaps the first book he had ever owned. How would he understand that a word had been left out? The seriousness of such a misprint cannot be exaggerated. Such an omission in a dictionary might lead to misunderstanding, but in a Bible it could imperil a man's immortal soul.

The edition was called in and burnt so that few 'Wicked' Bibles survive. Barker was ruined, and he bore the burden alone, for Bill was dead, leaving a young son. Norton, however, did not live long to rejoice: he died disgraced and in prison, while Barker struggled under a crushing load of debt. In 1634 the wretched man was compelled to lease the printing house, stock and equipment, and the patent itself, to that ruthless triumvirate, Miles Flesher, John Haviland and Robert Young (see p. 54).[11]

From the analysis in *Scintilla* of the misdeeds of those men it is clear that the great range of sizes of the Bible was the foundation of the huge profits they made. And it was Sparkes's exposure of their sharp practice that influenced Parliament, when it came to power, to oppose the monopoly of Bible printing. Puritans such as the Leveller, John Lilburne, cried out against 'this soul-starving or murdering monopoly'. 'Of all monopolies,' Lilburne declared, that of the Bible was 'most wicked and intolerable', for it deprived the poor of buying the book whereby they might be instructed 'in the way to heaven and happiness'.[12]

The Assembly of Divines who drew up the service book, the *Directory*, also considered the printing of the Bible. Four groups competed for their attention: the representative of the Barker family, Matthew Barker, who for years had been trying to buy out the trio; Flesher, after 1643 the surviving member of the original trio—though he had taken new partners; a group of eleven Stationers, who wanted a partnership like that in Jugge's time, and finally, the Company as a whole. After prolonged argument, the Company made agreements with Matthew Barker and with Flesher, and the eleven Stationers recognized defeat and tiptoed away.[13] John Bill's son was not involved, as yet. He had followed the King as a royal Printer, was declared a delinquent and taken prisoner with the Royalist cavalry in the West of England.

In 1645 the English Stock, which alone had the capital to

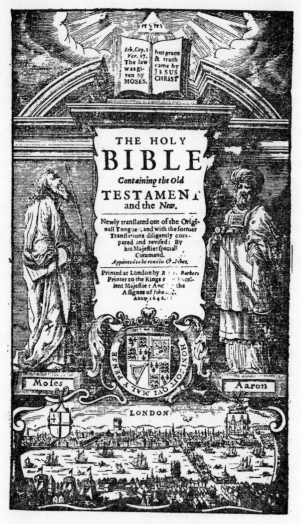

Fig. 21. Though the title page carries Robert
Barker's imprint, this Bible was printed by the
English Stock of the Stationers' Company.
Plate size $6\frac{15}{16} \times 4$ in.

operate the Printing House in Blackfriars, was issuing Bibles with the imprint of Robert Barker and the assigns of John Bill, but the rebels in the Company insisted that control should be taken from the Stock. The hard fact remained: the Stock had spent considerable sums and would have to be reimbursed. There was no alternative: if the English Stock was not to continue to finance the Bible patent, another Stock must be created. The truth of Christopher Barker I's statement as to the cost of Bible printing was proved once again. So in 1648 a Bible Stock came into existence.

Too much time had been spent in wrangling. As printing was still free from restrictions two outsiders had entered the field of Bible printing. The first, William Bentley, was probably in collusion with Christopher Barker III, son of the second Christopher, and with young John Bill.[14] Bentley was a more careful printer than his title-page suggests. The second outsider was John Field, a sort of ghost of Miles Flesher, for though a freeman of the Company he had taken no part in its activities, and it is not known how he obtained his considerable printing equipment. He had insinuated himself into an official appointment as Printer to the Parliament, and when Cromwell became Protector, Field became Printer to His Highness. Field was, in fact, bent on securing all that had belonged to the old King's Printer's patent. All these three groups began to publish Bibles in 1648 and 1649. Bitter rivalry and fierce price-cutting followed, and for the first time since Jugge's last days the English people had a choice of home-printed editions.

Another outsider joined Field; this was Henry Hills, who had once been a protégé of Lilburne, and had since become Printer to the Army. He was joined with Field as Printers to His Highness, and these two outwitted the Company's Bible Stock by a clever manoeuvre: they bought from Christopher Barker III and his uncle Matthew the actual manuscript of the original Authorized Version published in 1611. Protected by Cromwell, they entered their copy in the Stationers' register on March 6, 1656.[15] That was the end of the Bible Stock. Field and Hills were resolute in their efforts to suppress comprinting. Bentley was hounded by successive invasions of his printing house. Field secured from Cambridge the grant of their privilege, and the pair negotiated a covenant of forbearance with Oxford (see p. 59). Once again,

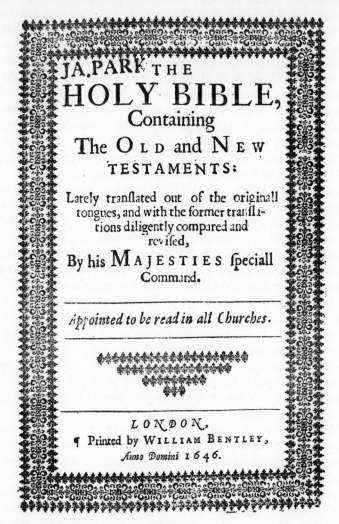

JA.PARK THE
HOLY BIBLE,
Containing
The Old and New TESTAMENTS:

Lately tranflated out of the originall
tongues, and with the former tranflì-
tions diligently compared and
revifed,

By his MAJESTIES fpeciall
Command.

Appointed to be read in all Churches.

LONDON,
¶ Printed by WILLIAM BENTLEY,
Anno Domini 1646.

Fig. 22. Page size $6\frac{1}{2} \times 4\frac{3}{8}$ in.

there was an absolute monopoly of Bible printing in this country.

At the Restoration Christopher Barker III and John Bill II applied to be reinstated in their patent. This was allowed. But once again the finance of the office was a decisive factor. Barker and Bill had no equipment, no stock and no capital. They secured orders to print, but they were forced to pass them to those who had been printing before the Restoration.[16] Field had retired to Cambridge before or soon after the return of Charles II, leaving Hills in partnership with another Stationer, Thomas Newcombe. These two, Hills and Newcombe, became the actual King's Printers, and moreover, they later acquired an interest in the patent itself. The imprints on Bibles and Proclamations no longer reveal the true state of affairs; the Barker and Bill families technically owned the patent until 1709, but in fact their interest had been split into a number of small shares.[17]

Hills was an extraordinary fellow: although he had been successively Printer to the Army, Printer to the Anabaptists, Printer to His Highness, Printer to the revived Rump Parliament, Printer to the revived Army and finally Printer to the Committee of Safety, he still managed to survive the Restoration. Not only so; but one of the first appointments to the royal household was that of Henry Hills, as Stationer—not Printer—to His Majesty. A contemporary remarked: ' . . . the man . . . has a soul of no common temper; he ever made it his business to be of the rising side; let what card would turn up trump he would still follow suit.'[18] Hills followed the example of Flesher and became a pillar of the Stationers' Company, and when the Vice-Chancellor of Oxford, Dr Fell, decided to comprint the privileged books, he faced the opposition of Henry Hills, not only as the wielder of the Bible patent but as a leading member of the Company determined to protect the English Stock. It was foolhardy of the Doctor, as yet inexperienced in the economics of publishing, to defy such a man.[19]

In 1673 Oxford embarked upon its first independent quarto Bible—the quarto size had then ceased to be the most popular. Hills and Newcombe retorted by printing the same size and drastically under-selling. They acknowledged that they lost £500, but they were able to recoup the loss by raising the prices of other sizes. Fell was warned that this would happen whatever size he printed. He was a determined man, not prepared easily to yield, but, after attempting in vain alone to combat Hills and New-combe, he sought help from those experienced in the trade: first two, and then four, London booksellers. They paid Fell £5,000 for books left on his hands, and advanced £3,000 so that the Bible printing in Oxford could go forward. Fell learnt the old lesson: that Bible printing needed capital.

The manoeuvre was successful. Bible prices tumbled, cut often by as much as 50 per cent, and so many were produced that the English colonies were able to buy from the home country instead of from Holland. The King's Printers protested to the King at the invasion of the patent, but he commanded them to take the matter to court, when the judgment was given in favour of Oxford.

That was not, however, the whole of the matter. Oxford needed the Singing Psalms to bind with its Bibles. The situation was one in which Bonham Norton would have revelled. The University's threat to comprint the Psalms would bring Henry Hills down to Oxford, in his capacity as Warden of the Company. He would insist that no agreement could be reached without bringing in the King's Printers. Then, as King's Printer, he would offer conditions impossible for Oxford to accept. Or the Company would agree to pay the University to forbear, and then obstruct the delivery of the Psalms so that Bible production was hindered. Suit followed suit in the Courts. The Stationers were reputed to be able to spend £200 a year on the defence of Stock copies, and Oxford was heavily penalized by legal costs whether the case were successful or not.

The bitterness which the Stationers brought to the struggle must be set in the context of their difficulties with L'Estrange as described in the previous chapter. Further, while they were engaged in the suppression of Oxford printing, they were themselves in danger of suppression by a Government that was attempting to break the power of the City.

Though Hills cleverly exploited his double role, he was chiefly disturbed that Oxford should comprint Bibles—the Singing Psalms were less important. It was the Bible patent around which all the quarrels revolved. Fell believed that costly as the printing was, the Bible offered the only means whereby the accounts of the learned press could be balanced. Hills and New-combe were determined that their profits should not be diminished by competition.

The accession in 1685 of the Roman Catholic James changed the situation slightly—and Hills had hurriedly to change his religion, and to forget that he had once sacked a man at the Blackfriars Printing House for being a Papist. The printing of the Authorized Version was no longer so favourably regarded by the Government. Hills obtained appointment as supplier of his Majesty's household and gained new profits by publishing Jesuit schoolbooks. This neatly evaded an infringement on the English Stock titles or the grammar patent.

The long and ingenious career of the versatile Hills was drawing to an end. In November 1688 William of Orange landed in this country. The Stationers hastily purged themselves of the Roman Catholic Hills, so closely associated with James, although he was then Warden of the Company. On the night James II fled, a mob raged into Blackfriars and set fire to the King's Printing House. Hills lost all his stock and equipment. He fled abroad and died shortly afterwards.

The appearance of William saved Oxford, and with Hills out of the way the University could reach agreement with the Londoners. The overriding licence of Oxford was acknowledged in respect to the Bible and the Book of Common Prayer. Cambridge drew automatic benefit from this arrangement, and from that time down to the present, the right of the two University Presses to share with the royal printers in the Authorized Version has not been contested.

Until 1709 the royal printing house in Blackfriars ran peacefully under Newcombe's successor as manager, one John Williams. But the adventures of the patent were by no means ended. The Hills-Newcombe term of thirty years was due to begin in 1710, and for about £2,300 their heirs sold a one-sixth interest to a London stationer, John Baskett (see Plate VII). Eventually, Baskett acquired the whole patent and its reversion. He is probably best known for his sumptuous Oxford folio, nicknamed the 'Basketful of errors', or the 'Vinegar' Bible, from a misprint for 'vineyard'. This may be typical of Baskett: that he had grand ideas but was a shade too hasty in the execution. He and Christopher Barker I were the only two shrewd businessmen who were able to exercise the patent alone, and Baskett only narrowly survived bankruptcy. He imitated the example of Flesher and Young in that he obtained a lease of Oxford's privilege in 1711 and a third-share of the Scottish patent. After the failure of the Stuart cause in 1715 Baskett strengthened his position in Scotland, for the unfortunate patentee had supported the Old Pretender.[20]

John Williams, an efficient and experienced Manager, must have been of material assistance to Baskett during the first ten years at Blackfriars. Nevertheless, Baskett had to mortgage his Oxford privilege and eventually sell the patent to Charles Eyre. The price, £10,000, was proportionately so much less than the price of Baskett's original one-sixth that he must have been hard pressed. On the other hand, Charles Eyre was a man to drive a hard bargain.

The Baskett family held the patent until 1769. They made no attempt to emulate the magnificent folio Bible printed at Cambridge by John Baskerville in 1763. It set a standard consistently ignored by London. There is no evidence that any royal printer has ever aspired to a superb Bible. Christopher Barker I printed well, but his typography was second-hand, as was his son's in the folio of 1611. No royal patentee could echo Baskerville's selfless statement: that the whole extent of his ambition was to print an octavo Book of Common Prayer and a folio Bible. Baskerville leased the Cambridge privilege under crippling restrictions, and did not attempt to make an economic success of large-scale Bible production.

Eyre was not a printer, and did not exercise the patent alone: he entered into partnership with William Strahan, a Scot who owned the largest printing house in late eighteenth-century London, and the King's Printing House was removed from Blackfriars to New Square, between Fleet Street and Holborn. Strahan had a long experience in the trade and was approved by no less a figure than Johnson, whose *Dictionary* had been printed at New Street. Neither Strahan nor Eyre was an idealist. They had bought the patent because it promised profits. Quick to see that a state of war demands innumerable documents, they were chiefly interested in Government printing during the decades of the struggles with America and France, and several printers in London and elsewhere were licensed to produce the Authorized Version.

At the beginning of the nineteenth century the net profits of

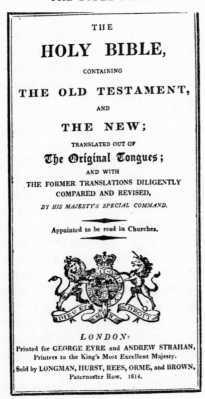

THE

HOLY BIBLE,

CONTAINING

THE OLD TESTAMENT,

AND

THE NEW;

TRANSLATED OUT OF

𝕿𝖍𝖊 𝕺𝖗𝖎𝖌𝖎𝖓𝖆𝖑 𝕿𝖔𝖓𝖌𝖚𝖊𝖘;

AND WITH

THE FORMER TRANSLATIONS DILIGENTLY
COMPARED AND REVISED,

BY HIS MAJESTY'S SPECIAL COMMAND.

Appointed to be read in Churches.

LONDON:
Printed for GEORGE EYRE and ANDREW STRAHAN,
Printers to the King's Most Excellent Majesty.
Sold by LONGMAN, HURST, REES, ORME, and BROWN,
Paternoster Row. 1814.

Fig. 23.
Page size
$4\frac{5}{8} \times 2\frac{5}{8}$ in.

the King's Printers were estimated as 216 per cent, something like £13,000. William Strahan, who had died in 1785, left a fortune of £100,000; his heir, Andrew, who died in 1831, left £800,000, excluding his estates.[21] But the public outcry against the huge expenditure on Government printing at last triumphed: this was taken away from the patent in the mid-century and given to Her Majesty's Stationery Office. The terms on which the patent was granted were altered so that the patentee now holds office, as judges do, 'quamdiu se bene gesserint'.

The demand for Bibles was vastly increased, first by the development of Sunday schools and secondly by the missionary societies. The British and Foreign Bible Society, founded in 1804, and the Edinburgh Bible Society, a few years younger, offered new markets. After about 1814 the patentees, who later became Eyre and Spottiswoode, undertook a vigorous publishing

programme, and there was intense competition between them and
the two University Presses to gain very large orders for very cheap
Bibles. Successful stereotyping, using the plaster-of-paris
mould to make an exact printing plate from type, was promoted
by the Bible printers (see p. 209). The high cost of the process
could be offset by the advantage of using the same plate for very
large editions.

Towards the end of the century, the two Universities jointly
undertook the preparation of a Revised Version. The expense was
considerable, for there were 407 meetings of the revisers before
the Old Testament appeared in 1881 and the New Testament
three years later. This version, it was held, did not come under
the patent, but was the copyright of the revisers and their publishers—thus, it was prudent to choose at least one reviser for
youth rather than scholarship! This may or may not have been the
true legal interpretation of the patent, but the royal printers
wisely did not recourse to law; wisely, because the Revised Version
has never achieved the popularity of the Authorized Version, for
all the scholarship employed. Typographically, the first edition
was a careful but uninspired piece of Victorian printing.

Indeed, although many versions of the Bible have since been
offered to the public, although there is recurrent dissatisfaction
with the Authorized Version, the work of the translators of 1611
has not yet been supplanted in the churches or in the affection of
the nation. Until the second world war the printing house round
New Square continued to supply the Authorized Version to
uncounted churches and to the homes of Bible readers throughout the world.

Since the second world war there has been no Bible printing in
London. Eyre and Spottiswoode's house was destroyed and not
rebuilt, for there was no obligation on the patentees to print in the
capital, and the King's Printers (as they then were) had survived
as book printers in London when many of their contemporaries,
unsupported by the never-ceasing orders for the Bible, had been
forced to emigrate to the suburbs or the provinces.

Since the demand for cheap Bibles, competitively produced,
the profits in Bible printing have not been sufficient to attract
infringement of the patent, and no prudent English book printer
is likely to attempt it. Nor has the existence of the patent prevented
the publication in recent years of certain fine or limited editions,

for these do not compete with the business of the patentees. The practical operation of the patent has been continuously modified since the sixteenth century; yet unaltered in theory, it did successfully survive into twentieth-century London as the sole representative of the system that once dominated the London printing trade.

The Bible printers, who since 1611 have been producing volumes the contents of which have remained virtually unchanged, are one extreme of the range of London printing. At the other are the periodical printers, the contents of whose publications, if daily, are totally changed every twenty-four hours, Yet, as will seen in the next chapter, problems were shared, and the greatest typographical benefit conferred on Bible printers in recent years was the type face designed on the site of the former King's Printing House for a newspaper: The Times New Roman.

NOTES

1 No patent has survived. There is a reproduction from a well-executed Proclamation of Faques in E. G. Duff, *Wynkyn de Worde and his Contemporaries* (London, 1925).

2 There is no patent for Berthelet, only an authorization for his salary as King's Printer (£4) in the Public Record Office (Patent roll 21 Henry VIII, pt 2, m. 17; C 66/655).

3 Richard Grafton to Thomas Cromwell, ? end of August 1537, B.M., Cotton MSS., Cleopatra E v, f. 340.

4 The patent of Cawood and Jugge is in the P.R.O. (Patent roll 19 Elizabeth, m. 38; C 66/944).

5 There is an account of these agreements and combinations in Liber A of the Stationers' Company under June 9, 1575 (Bib. Soc. transcript).

6 Christopher Barker I's patent is printed in Hansard's *Typographia* (London, 1825).

7 Christopher Barker's account of the privileges is printed in Arber i, 114–16.

8 William Jackson, *Records of the Court of the Stationers' Company* (London, Bib. Soc., 1957), under July 14, 1606.

9 This information comes from a document printed by Arber, iv, 11. The author, a biographer of one of the translators, implies that the Company paid the costs, but he was not in a position to understand the relationship between the Company and the King's Printer. It is highly improbable that the Company would have paid such a bill.

10 The feet of fine in the P.R.O. (19 Jas I, Trinity) show that Norton and Bill paid a fine of £300 for Hunsdon House. In 1629 Bill described the King's Printing House (P.R.O., C 2 Chas I, B. 118. 44). The transactions leading up to the publication of the 'wicked' Bible in 1631 are fully described in *The 'Wicked' Bible and the King's Printing House, Blackfriars*, privately printed for The Times Publishing Company (1958).

11 This lease and the efforts of the Barker family to regain possession are described in State Papers Domestic, 1644, 503, part 2.

12 J. Lilburne, *England's Birthright* (October 1645). See William M. Clyde, 'Parliament and the Press, II', *The Library* (1933–4), xiv, 39.

13 The negotiations for the Bible monopoly occupied the Court of the Company from February 19, 1644, when they began seriously to treat, and January 15, 1646, when the English Stock reported its production of Bibles (Bibliographical Society photostats).

14 Bentley's association with the former patentees is stated in a post-Restoration report on the state of King's Printers' Patent (P.R.O., State Papers Domestic, 29.16.41). In November 1656 Bentley published an account of his case (B.M., Thomason Collection), and in the reply of Field and Hills was accused of being a figurehead.

15 *The London Printers Lamentation, or, the Press oppressed and overpressed* (? 1660), printed in Arber, iii, 27.

16 See P.R.O., State Papers Domestic, 29.16.42.

17 Robert Haig, 'New Light on the King's Printing Office 1680–1730', *Studies in Bibliography* (University of Virginia, 1956), viii, 157.

18 There is a lively account of Henry Hills in *The Life of H.H. Printer* (London, 1688).

19 John Johnson and Strickland Gibson, *Print and Privilege at Oxford to the year 1700* (Oxford, 1946). The internal difficulties of the Stationers' Company are described by Cyprian Blagden, 'Charter Trouble', *The Bookcollector* (Winter, 1957), 369.

20 D. Lee, *Memorial for the Bible Societies of Scotland* (Edinburgh, 1824).

21 Samuel Brooke, *An Appeal to the Legislature on the subject of the Office of King's Printer in England* (London, 1830).

G

IV

The Periodical Press:
Sixteenth and Seventeenth Centuries

THIS account of printing in London has so far concentrated on the book trade, which until the end of the seventeenth century was dominated by the privileges and patents. When we turn to periodical publications we are in a different world. There is no more of those two giants, John Day and William Seres, there is nothing about the English Stock and the Court of Assistants. In the sixteenth and seventeenth centuries the periodical publications—which were usually of news—were known as 'small copies', and they were produced by 'small' printers and booksellers. During these two centuries there was no general and insatiable demand for news as there was for grammars, primers and books of private prayer. Consequently, the interests of the news publishers were not shared by the main body of the Stationers' Company.

News publications differ basically from those handled by the book trade, but it was only slowly understood in what way they were different. Today it is obvious that a periodical publication differs in format from a book, and that it does so because it must be printed and distributed at regular intervals; the shorter the intervals the greater the distinction in format. Because these publications must be produced regularly, the price must be kept low; the more frequent the intervals, the lower the price. It is periodicity that distinguishes newspapers, journals, magazines, reviews and even some annuals from books and from jobbing (posters, cards, tickets, etc.), and it is periodicity that dictates format and price.

Moreover, a periodical publication is distinguished from a book or a piece of jobbing because it is dated and numbered. By giving this information the publisher indicates that at a certain interval the next number will appear. The method of dating often reveals this interval: daily, weekly, monthly or quarterly. The number identifies the place in the series and also serves as a promise by the publisher to produce further numbers.

It was not easy for the early printers and booksellers in London to make these distinctions: there was no precedent for periodical publishing, since the printing press alone makes possible the mass multiplication at high speed that is the essence of the business. Periodical publishing had to be invented, and it was not invented all at once. The newspaper came first, because it is the nature of news to be published periodically.

There was a precedent for the compilation of news items. Before the printing press was invented and for nearly two centuries afterwards, news of battles, prices of commodities, royal marriages and natural disasters was made known to a limited circle either by letter or by messenger. Before and during the medieval period this circle was restricted to the ruler and his immediate servants or deputies. During the fifteenth century in Europe another class obtained power, the politicians, bankers and merchants. They appreciated the value of news and to have it they organized a service by arranging for agents to write to them. The establishment of such a manuscript service antedates the first printed news publication.

This appeared comparatively early in this country, though it was not a newspaper but a newsbook—distinction in format was not understood. The publication is not dated or numbered: the publisher was not planning to issue such publications regularly, he was making no contract with the customer. The format was that of a book of those times, twelve pages, $7\frac{1}{2}$ by 5 inches, with the type, a book face in book size, set to the full measure, as in a book. The printer may well have been occupied more in the display of his crude ornaments than in publishing news: page 1 appears to show an early use in this country of decorative units cast in metal, not cut in wood (see Fig. 24).[1]

Richard Faques, the printer-publisher—son of William Faques, the King's Printer—had no precedent to follow when he planned the title of his publication, and sensibly he offered a summary of the contents: 'Hereafter ensue the true encounter or battle lately

¶ Hereafter ensue the trewe encounter or... ¶ Batayle latelp don betwene . Englande and: Scotlande. In whiche batayle the . Scottis-he .Kynge was Nayne.

¶ The maner of thadua̅cesynge of my lord of Surrey tresourier and . Marshall of . Englande and leuetenu̅te generall of the north pties of th e same With . xxvi . M̅ . men to Wardes the kyn-ge of . Scottis and his . Armye veWed and nom/bred to an / hundred thousande men at / theleest.

Fig. 24. Page 1 of the *Trewe Encounter*, 1513.
Size of wood block 2⅞ × 4 in.

done between England and Scotland, in which battle the Scottish King was slain.' The word 'lately' should be noted, for we still buy the 'late' editions of the morning or evening newspapers because we want the latest reports. The price of this little news-book was not mentioned: it was possibly fourpence, the groat, a fourpenny piece, being then a common unit of coinage.

Although the *Trewe Encounter* is not a periodical publication, it deserves attention as a publication of news. Faques understood as well as Lord Northcliffe that the public would be eager to buy an account of the battle of Flodden, fought on September 9, 1513. He put together an eye-witness report of the battle, a list of Scots casualties and a list of the English who had distinguished them-selves in the fighting—exactly the contents of a modern newspaper report. Then, to make the production attractive to the, perhaps, semi-literate customer, he added a news picture on the front page. The block may not have been cut specially for the occasion, but it is full of action, with men hewing vigorously at one another. The man coming out of the tent with the crown in his hand appeals to our enduring interest in royalty.

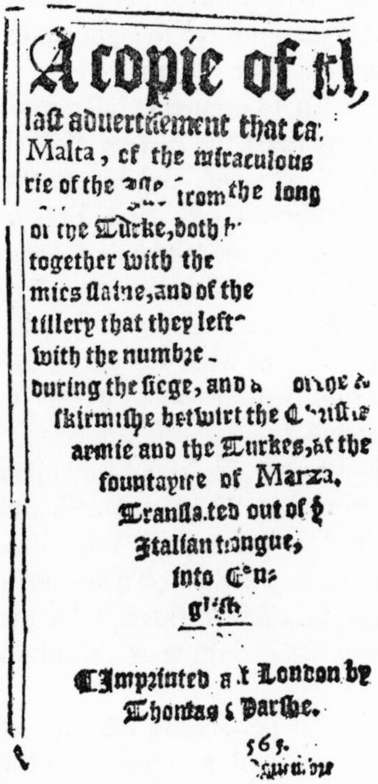

This newsbook survives only in fragments, of which one sheet was only recently discovered and by accident, for it had been used to bind another book.[2] Other examples may yet be discovered, but so far as is known, the venture was not continued by Faques or imitated by others for many years. A later example is an early 'tabloid', only about 5 by 3½ inches, of which only fragments survive. It was published in 1565 by Thomas Marsh, and was not a home-produced article as Faques' had been but a translation from an Italian publication. The long title includes the word 'advertisement', then beginning to be used as the exact equivalent of our 'news'.[3]

A copie of t[

laſt aduertiſement that ca:
Malta, of the miraculous
rie of the ꝛꝫe from the long
o₁ tpe Turke, both h·
together with the
mies ſlaine, and of the
tillery that they left·
with the numbꝛe .
during the ſiege, and ↄ onꝛge ↄ
ſkirmiſhe betwixt the C·ꝛiſtiↄ
armie and the Turkes, at the
fountapire of Marza,
Tranſla.ted out of ꝫ
Italian tongue,
into Cꝛnꝛ
g'·ſh

¶ Impꝛinted a.t London by
Thomas ꝫ Marſhe.
565.
ꝛauꝛ.bꝛ

Fig. 25. Page size 5 × 3½ in.

Italy was the great centre of news gathering throughout the sixteenth century. The private manuscript newsletters originated there, where they were produced on some scale for the bankers and merchants. English statesmen, such as Lord Burghley, Queen Elizabeth's principal minister, would subscribe to a service, for instance from Venice. At that city, items from all over Europe would be collected and set down under headings of the name of each town.[4] Such newsletters were not signed or addressed, but were supplied by contract. Statesmen would also arrange for letters that were addressed to them personally, 'my humble duty remembered to your Lordship', or whatever was appropriate, and signed by the agent. Home news would be supplied by a London bookseller, who would employ a professional writer or scribe, a leftover from the original Stationers' Company, to collect together the items from the town that were to be sent out to subscribers.[5]

The format of these letters was consistent: a folio sheet, folded once to produce four pages, the last of which would be left blank for the direction. The Italian letters sometimes ran to eight pages, one section being folded inside the other for the post.

The English Government first began to secure regular news when Sir Francis Walsingham systematized the receipt of such 'intelligence' or 'advertisements', that is 'news', and his system was brought to perfection by Sir Robert Cecil, first Earl of Salisbury.[6] It is fashionable to describe the agents of these ministers as 'spies'; it would be as incorrect and invidious to call Mr Alastair Cooke or 'Our Own Correspondent' a spy. 'Intelligencers' were paid correspondents who sent what we would call 'news' and their reports contain much that we would expect to find in the columns of *The Times* today.

Men in power, men engaged in commerce, could not rely upon the spasmodic sort of thing being printed by Thomas Marsh and others. There was, however, a demand for printed news developing among people who could not afford to pay their own agents or even to subscribe to the booksellers. Gradually, throughout the sixteenth century the periodical press was emerging as a result of the growing demand for news.

Before the end of the century printed newsbooks like that of Faques or Marsh were both numerous and popular. For the twenty years between 1590 and 1610 over 250 survive and the titles of nearly 200 more are known from the entries in the Stationers' register.[7] If these figures are averaged out, they give a newsbook once a fortnight, and if the newsbooks had indeed appeared regularly from one publisher, he would have been forced to date and number his publications in order to provide some means of distinguishing between them.

There was no single publisher, and publication was far from regular. The books were wholly dependent on events, and when there was no event, or report of it, no book appeared. In most cases the books contained only one report from a single source. The foreign news had considerable range: battles, troop movements, treaties, royal marriages, births and deaths, but the

English Government banned all home news except for trivial items such as natural disasters, monstrous births, executions, public festivities or royal speeches. Nothing controversial could be published; it would not be licensed.

Further, many of these books did not contain authentic 'news'. The ballad form was popular, as it was certain to be with a population so generally illiterate, and though the 'woeful lamentation' of a condemned man may claim to be 'news' in that it was published at the earliest moment, it was no more authentic than other utterances from the condemned cell which have entertained the public ever since. Offenders separated both by space and time would produce an identical lamentation.

The ballad form was also popular because the customers upon whom the publishers relied liked to be entertained as well as informed. They were not so serious in their demand for accurate news as the statesmen and financiers who subscribed to the manuscript news services. Thus, illustration was necessary in the printed newsbooks if a circulation of any size were to be secured. But blocks were expensive, and so they were used time and again —after all, one fire is much like another fire, and one execution like another except to the central figure. [8]

The format continued to be that of a book. There was a title-page with a blank verso and the news began on page 3. It was set out with decorative initials and pieces of type ornament as a book would have been. The title was still a summary of the contents: 'True News' was not the equivalent of our *Daily News*.

At the end of the century appeared the first man to perceive that the periodical press was radically different from the book trade. That man was John Wolfe, who is the father of news publishing, though not, as it proved, of perodical journalism. He was a man of extraordinary interest. Like so many Elizabethans he was hugely ambitious—no doubt, he prayed earnestly to remain in prosperity—and to gain his ends he pursued a devious path that may well have been carefully planned.

He began with few advantages for he was not the son of the celebrated printer Reinold Wolfe, who was one of the original members of the reconstituted Stationers' Company. His father was probably a City fishmonger, though a wealthy tradesman. Young John was apprenticed to Day, and afterwards was so keenly interested that he travelled abroad to study printing. [9] He returned from the Continent bursting with enthusiasm, eager to practise, and found the London trade was controlled by the powerful patent-holders. Not content to be a back-street printer, he began openly to attack the Company, with, as has been described (see p. 39), a certain success.

There can be little doubt that he had raised the flag of revolt for reasons other than altruism. He happily accepted the share in Day's patent, became an official of the Company, and was thereafter to be found searching out unlicensed printing and seizing presses with all the zeal of a convert. What is more important is that he himself owned more presses than anyone except the Queen's Printer, and he managed to set them up actually in Stationers' Hall, an enviably central position and adjacent to that mart of news, St Paul's, where the gossip-mongers, merchants and citizens met to exchange reports.

Such drive and enterprise in the man were likely to secure success in news publication. Wolfe seems to have begun the large-scale publishing of news about 1589. In that year he owed a considerable sum for entered copies, probably small ones like newsbooks, which he was either in too great a hurry to pay for or else hoped to avoid paying for—as, in the end, he did.[10]

Wolfe made no fundamental changes in the format adopted by Richard Faques more than seventy years before, the format of the book. Two points, however, are of importance. Wolfe did strive to standardize the layout of the title-page, so that his productions are distinguishable from those of his contemporaries. This adherence to a formula, basically recognizable, upon which changes can be rung is of first importance in periodical publications. Secondly, he began to standardize the title itself—a most important development because it leads directly to the naming of a publication, a respect in which a periodical obviously differs from a book.

Unlike his contemporaries and immediate successors, Wolfe stripped his title-page. This page, which in the newsbook was the equivalent of the modern masthead (carrying the name and other details, at the top of page 1 of a newspaper), in his hands began to be a front page that typographically informed the customer he was buying 'John Wolfe's news'. He ceased to pack the space with details of contents: there was only the short title, the house block and the imprint. Lord Beaverbrook follows a similar formula, block and all, in the masthead of the *Daily Express*. Incidentally, for French news Wolfe would use a block that included a fleur-de-lys, one of those imaginative touches in major and minor matters that contributed to his success (see Plate IX). He was deflected from these interesting typographical experiments, which would have accelerated the career of periodical printing, when he became Printer to the City in 1593.

These devices on the title-page were most effective on the smaller newsbooks. When these publications consisted of only eight pages the two signatures were generally side-stitched and the title-page was page 1. But larger newsbooks often had a blank wrapper, which kept the book clean but concealed the title-page from the customer.

Wolfe was, however, far more than a printer of news: he had a contribution to make to the technique of obtaining news. His appreciation of the value of this commodity must have been stimulated by his travels, particularly in Italy where it is known he spent some years. These travels provided him with useful contacts and in his publications he used not only letters that may have been addressed to him personally, but several times he published translations of French and Italian printed sheets that may have been provided by his friends abroad.

In those contacts he had two sources: but the frequent publication of news demands several, and these he proceeded to organize. Thus, some of his newsbooks carry on the title-page the legend 'Published by Authority'—a statement that is today the prerogative of the *London Gazette*, as it has been since Restoration times. The Elizabethan Government was far from eager to sponsor the publication of news, and indeed permitted only the most innocuous items to trickle to the press. Wolfe's assertion was almost impudent, but he would not have dared to use it had he not good warrant.

A note attached to one of his entries in the Stationers' register may hint at how he accomplished this *coup*: 'By order of the Council [the Queen's Privy Council] certified under Master Wilkes his hand.'[11] Thomas Wilkes was not only Clerk of the Privy Council and an experienced diplomat, but a man with an interest in printing, for he had once possessed a royal patent which he sold to Christopher Barker I. He was, possibly, hard pressed for money: at any rate, if Wolfe had offered him hard cash to allow him to print manuscript news that came either to the Clerk or to the Council and to license the printing, Wilkes might well agree. It would be worth a good deal to Wolfe to be able to make that attractive claim that his news was 'published by authority'. Wilkes was, as it were, the Foreign Office spokesman of the day.

Lastly, Wolfe used other letters that were apparently from private persons on a mission abroad, and these were probably bought from the recipient. One of these correspondents is identified by the initials TB, which almost certainly stand for Thomas Barnes, so providing another glimpse of Wolfe's enterprise, for Thomas Barnes has his equivalent today in Reuter's correspondents. He was the paid agent of Thomas Phelippes, who has acquired notoriety as the decipherer of the letters of Mary Queen of Scots when she was a prisoner in England, as a result of which his career has been much misrepresented. In fact, he was the leading—and only—news editor of the day. Members of the Government who required a service of manuscript newsletters took it from Phelippes. He developed his service on a vast scale and eventually went bankrupt to the sum of thousands of pounds, fabulous money in those days.

The arrangements were simple: Phelippes had paid agents like Barnes, who either went abroad and sent back reports to Phelippes or who set down at his direction news from England to be sent abroad in exchange. The fruits of this service were then supplied to someone in high office. In 1592 Phelippes devoted his service to the Earl of Essex, and later he worked for Sir Robert Cecil, but at the time when Wolfe was strenuously engaged in news publishing Phelippes was without a patron, and would, no doubt, have been willing to sell items, such as the letters from Thomas Barnes, to the London news printer.[12]

Wolfe's supply, therefore, may have come from sources that were almost identical with those of our own day: the republishing of foreign news items from printed papers, the official announcements, the private correspondents and contacts and the agency reports.

Though Wolfe was a superb manager, who would have been successful today, he was no editor—it is probable that no man can be both. For instance, the letters from TB would be printed unabridged. The opening was personal: 'My good friend, the

The befeeging of Paris by the King, and Mounficur de Chaillllon with 1000, horfe, & 3000 fote-men,lyeth in the fraburbs on the one fide, & the Vice-count di Turena,in another of the fruburbes on the other fide, in the behalfe of the king.

The execution of three Traitours bes ing two friends a priest, that had con-iured murder the king.

The Citie of Saint Denis yielded to the king, where his Maieftie maketh abiderit.

Fig. 26. Double-spread illustration in a John Wolfe newsbook of 1591. Block size 4×9 in.

manifold courtesies by me sundry ways received at your hands makes me not unkindful of you.' This is Barnes thanking Phelippes. Or Barnes may refer 'to our last conference together at your lodging', when he and Phelippes had talked with a gentleman who had travelled in France. John Wolfe's customers would have been much mystified by these allusions; John Wolfe ought to have edited them out of the letter. Perhaps it did not occur to him; perhaps he thought that he, a mere news publisher, should not touch the immortal prose of a journalist; or perhaps he felt that he had paid good money and every word should be used. He would, indeed, have been far in advance of his time had he turned his hand to sub-editing, for in the end pressure on space rather than a sense of what was appropriate drove his successors to cut reports.[13]

Wolfe was aware of the importance of illustration and like his contemporaries he had blocks cut that could be used again and again. But here again he showed his lively imagination. Once he included a map of a battle, which was printed separately and appears to have been used as the outside wrapper (i.e. A1). The block was not new and showed the siege of a sea-coast fort—inappropriate to a newsletter about the siege of a Paris suburb; but there was plenty of smoke pouring from the guns, and the scene was made vivid for the reader. On another occasion he was more

TO THE READER.

East that the better forte shoulde be mif-ledde by the malicious, who hearing of fome fmal garboyl betweene the French and Eng-lifh, enlarged it fo on Tenter-hookes, that they proclaimed it a ruin of both the armies. I thought it good to publifh this Iournall *of* Aduertifements, *which I receaued out of* Brittanie*, as well to make it knowen how well our flender and weake Forces daylie confront the enemie, as alfo with what good agreement (by the great wifdome of the Commaunders) the two* Naeions *ioyne in a common quarrell againft a common enemie.*

If I may finde this to be acceptable to the Reader, I fhall be willing to acquaint him with the reft, as it fhall come vnto my handes.

Farewell.

A 3

Fig. 27. John Wolfe's announcement published in October 1591. Measure 18½ picas, type depth (excluding signature) 4 in.

ambitious: the illustration of a multiple execution took up the double-page spread. So big a block was possibly cut in segments, and it is, of course, possible that parts could be used for other executions. The clumsy captions suggest another use. As the block was printed on a separate sheet which was not backed up, Wolfe could easily have run off extra copies and sold the sheets as a publication separate from the newsbook. There would be a market among the semi-literate or illiterate for a grisly picture rendered in unsparing detail.

Lastly, Wolfe began to approach the idea of publishing period-ically. In 1591 he made an announcement to his readers, typo-graphically a pleasant piece of work, with several niceties such as a tapered setting, an alternation of roman with italic, and tolerable presswork—only one jumped-up space; Wolfe was a conscientious craftsman. But the importance of the announce-ment lies in its last sentence: 'If I may find this to be acceptable to the Reader, I shall be willing to acquaint him with the rest, as it shall come unto my hands.' He was on the verge of making a contract with the reader. He had already been driven to date his publications, although the date was that of the news, not of pub-lication; had he continued he might have been forced to number his publications and to state the day of issue, and so the periodical press would have come into existence.

But he did not continue with news publishing. It was soon after this issue that he became Printer to the City and devoted himself to job printing. Nevertheless, he had made more progress in five years than his predecessors made in seventy. There is the stand-ardization not only of layout but of title, the exploitation of many sources of news, the production of illustration that really did illustrate the report, and the hint at regular, periodical publishing. He had given tremendous impetus to the evolution of the periodical press, with its complex structure utterly different from the book trade.

Wolfe's travels abroad had helped him to appreciate news publishing since other countries were well advanced. On the Continent the winged god Mercury who carried messages was associated with the first named newsbook, *Mercurius Gallobelgicus*, begun in 1594. The notion of speed in bringing news to the public was not aptly applied to this publication—it was a bi-annual. In Germany dated news pamphlets were being published in 1609 in Wolfenbüttel and Strasbourg, though few survive. In Holland there were dated news sheets from 1618. In 1620 an English translation of a Dutch news sheet was being printed in Amster-dam for distribution in London.[15]

This country lagged behind. No frequently appearing news publication was openly printed in London until September 1621, when a short series was commenced. The newsbook format was not used: instead, the Dutch custom of a single small sheet was introduced, but seems not to have been popular, necessary development though it was. Not until May 23, 1622, was the first successful series begun, and this reverted to the newsbook format. The names of Nicholas Bourne and Thomas Archer, both booksellers, appeared in the first imprints, but later the name of the man who undoubtedly was the force behind this series was added: Nathaniel Butter.

Butter was one of the more attractive figures in the London printing trade. He was an experienced stationer and from the few records that survive it seems likely that he led the trade in the promotion of new ideas. There was that bright idea he had had in 1611 to have the primer printed abroad and secretly imported to London, an idea that had brought down the wrath of the Company upon his head (see p. 47). As a result Butter had come to rely on small copies, such as William Shakespeare's *King Lear*, and for many years before 1622 he had published newsbooks, sensational and serious, whenever a report came to hand. Bourne had no such record; nor had Archer. The short series of 1621 had been printed for 'NB' and the most eminent modern authorities believe that the initials stood for Nathaniel Butter—Bourne's, of course, were also NB.[16] However, the records reveal Bourne as a cautious man, who would be likely to adopt an idea when it had been tested and proved successful; when it was no longer successful he dropped it.

It was necessary in the conditions of the time that several booksellers should participate in publication: for instance, this would make it easier to find a printer. It was a crippling restriction on the development of the periodical press that no printer could have more than two or three presses. And indeed, the periodical press did not flourish until restrictions were lifted from the printing trade.

Butter has the title—perhaps to be shared with Bourne—of father of the periodical press. He has this honour rather than Wolfe because it is with this series of Butter and Bourne that dating and numbering begin, the dating and numbering that are fundamental to periodical publishing. Butter, with his considerable experience of news publishing, was better placed than Bourne to perceive distinctions, to understand that periodical publications must differ from books: and so, the periodical press was born.[17]

Nouem. 7. 1622. *Numb. 6.*

A Coranto.

RELATING

DIVERS PARTICV-LARS CONCERNING
THE NEWES OVT OF *ITALY,*
Spaine, *Turkey*, *Persia*, *Bohemia*, *Sweden*, *Poland*, *Austria*, the *Pallatinates*, the *Grisons*, and divers places of the Higher and Lower GERMANIE.

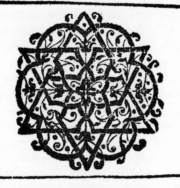

Printed for *Nathaniel Butter*, *Nicholas Bourne*, and *William Shefford*, 1622.

Fig. 28. Page size $7\frac{1}{2} \times 5\frac{1}{2}$ in.

Dating with the day of publication was adopted from the opening of the series on May 23, 1622, but numbering appears to have been adopted almost accidentally. On October 15, 1622, there was occasion for two issues, one a continuation of a previous packet of news, the other separate in content. Here was the opportunity for a man with bright ideas: to put No. 1 on the first and No. 2 on the second. Whether this idea came to Butter, which one favours, or to Bourne, they were shrewd men and could see how convenient numbering was, both for themselves and their customers. After missing one issue, they adopted the practice consistently and it has been continued ever since. Thus, the contract with the reader came into being.[18]

Otherwise, Butter and Bourne made no great changes. The format remained that of a book, with the title-page, blank verso, news on page 3. The page size remained the same, about $7\frac{1}{2}$ by $5\frac{3}{4}$ inches, roughly that of the *Concise Oxford Dictionary* today. Their newsbooks contained more pages than Wolfe's, usually twenty or twenty-four, and they appeared frequently, at least once a week, though not upon days that were formally announced.

The title was still a summary of the contents and changed with each issue: logically, if you argue that the contents were always different. The repetition of certain words such as Coranto, Relation, News or Continuation served, however, to distinguish newsbooks from all other books, and in 1625 the title *Mercurius Britannicus* was introduced for a short period to identify the publications; it was actually the name of the publishing syndicate, however, and not of their production. It is surprising that they failed to realize how helpful a consistently used name would have been, and the more surprising since Butter, when he entered the copies in the Stationers' register, simply put 'A currant (i.e. coranto) of news'.[19] We know from contemporary references that the customer asked for the latest currant or coranto. Thus, the idea of the named newsbook was implicit, but not yet explicit on the title-page.

The contemporary manuscript newsletter influenced the publishers in many ways. Typographically it was recalled by the centre heading of the place or origin and the date of the original letter where we would expect to find a headline. There was no sub-editing or abridgement: the manuscript original was printed in entirety, with expressions such as 'loving friend' left in, although

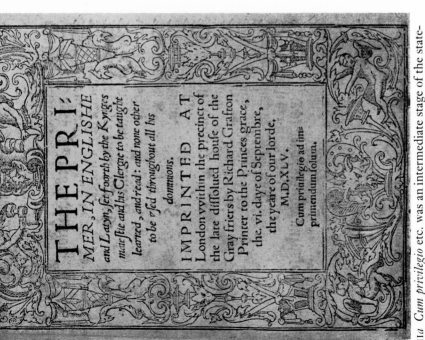

b The single-sheet hornbook alphabet, type size about 16 point, was a profitable monopoly. (See p. 39; 3½ × 2⅜ in.)

11*a* *Cum privilegio* etc. was an intermediate stage of the statement denoting monopoly. (See p. 26; page size, 7½ × 5 in.)

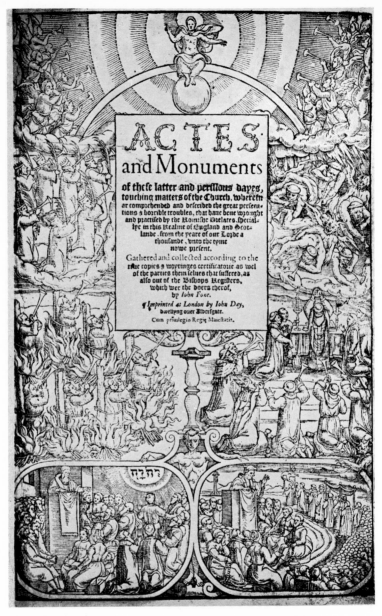

III The handsome title page of Foxe's popular account of the English Protestant martyrs is typical of the high quality of Day's printing. (See p. 34; page size, $12\frac{1}{2} \times 7\frac{3}{4}$ in.)

FRANCISCI
DE VERULAMIO,
Summi Angliæ
CANCELLARII,
Instauratio
magna.

Multi pertransibunt & augebitur scientia.

Sur Pass sculp.

LONDINI
Apud Joannem Billium,
Typographum
Regium.

Anno   1620

IV The engraved title page, of which this is an unusually fine
example, was well established in London by 1620. (See
p. 50; plate size, $9\frac{1}{4} \times 5\frac{13}{16}$ in.)

LILIES RVLES construed.

Whereunto are added
T H O. R O B I N S O N S
Heteroclites, the Latine
Syntaxis, and
Qui mihi.

Whereunto are now also added
the Rules for the Genders of Nounes,
and Preterperfect Tenses and Su-
pines of Verbs in En-
glish alone.

L O N D O N,

Printed by R O G E R N O R T O N Printer
to the Kings most Excellent Maiesty,
in Latine, Greeke, and Hebrew. 1638.

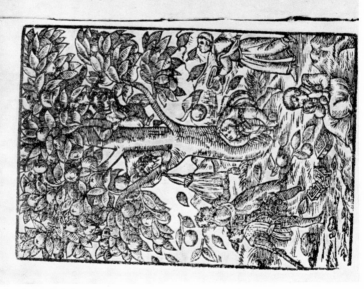

v This edition of the Latin
Grammar associated with
William Lillie was printed
when Roger Norton was leas-
ing his grammar patent to
Flesher, Haviland and Young.
(See p. 54; page size, $5\frac{3}{4} \times 3\frac{1}{2}$
in.)

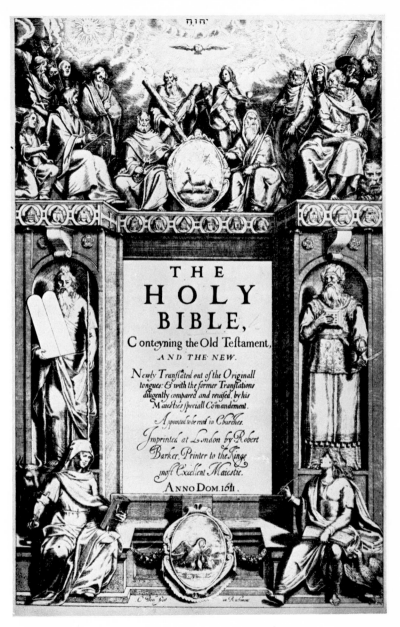

VI Cornelius Boel engraved the title page for the first folio edition of King James's Bible. (See p. 81; plate size, 13¾ × 8⅞ in.)

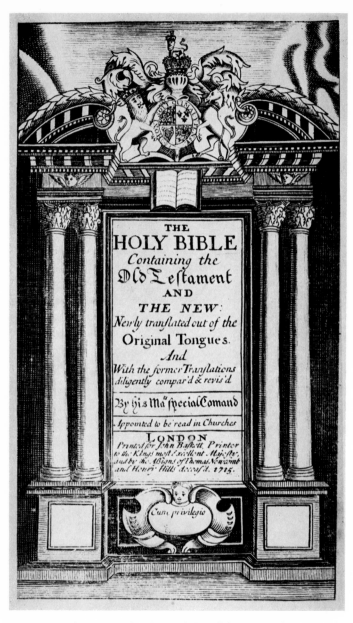

VII John Baskett secured a share of the Bible patent of Newcombe and Hills whose thirty-year term began in 1709. (See p. 91; plate size, $6\frac{7}{8} \times 4$ in.)

True Newes,

Concerning the win=
ning of the Towne of *Corbeyll*
by the French King from the Prince of Parma.

Which was docne on S. Martins *euen*
at night laft paft. 1590.

Sent from Deepe to an English Gentleman.

AT LONDON
Prinnted by *E. A.* and are to
be folde at the little North doore of
Paules Church at the figne
of the Gunne.
1590.

VIII The title of a newsbook referred to the subject, not to
periodical publication, and the date was that of the single
news item. (See p. 103; page size, 7 × 5 in.)

CREDIBLE

Reportes from France,
and Flanders. In the moneth
of May. 1590.

LONDON
Printed by John Wolfe, and are to be solde by
William Wright.
1590.

Aduertisements
FROM THE LOVV
Countries.

The 16. *day of* October.

LONDON
Printed by Iohn Wolfe. *Anno Domini*
1591.

Aduertisements
FROM BRITANY,
And from the Lovv Countries.

In September and October.

LONDON
Printed by Iohn Wolfe. *Anno Domini,*
1591.

IX These three Wolfe title pages show the beginning of the mast-head development that is mature in Plate X. (See p. 104; page size, 7 × 5 in.)

Though the mid-seventeenth century *Mercurius Civicus*
is small compared with the eighteenth-century papers,
these were less than one-quarter of the page size of *The Times*
our own day.

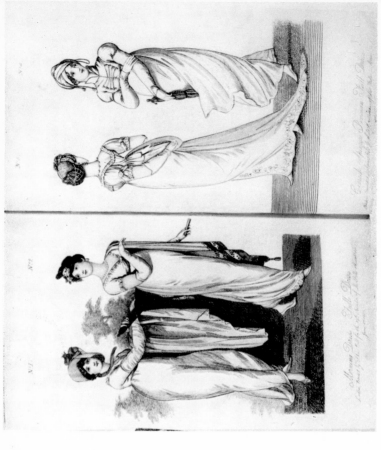

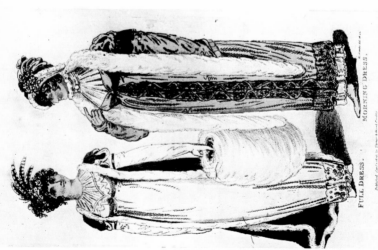

XI*a* and *b*. The two rigid models (left) of the late-eighteenth-century fashion plates in the *Ladies' Monthly Museum* developed into the four vivacious models of *La Belle Assemblée*, early nineteenth-century. All such plates were coloured. (See pp. 145, 151, page size,

View of the Pneumatic Railway in operation, with trains on a double line passing a station.

Sectional view of the Railway Cylinder showing the internal arrangement.

XIIa During the early-Victorian railway boom the engraved plates in periodicals devoted to the subject reached a high standard of craftsmanship. (See p. 160; *Railway Magazine* of 1835; plate size, $2\frac{7}{8} \times 8\frac{13}{16}$ in.)

b The casting box, probable height about four feet, that curved stereotype plates was developed in the Office of *The Times*.

XIII The engraver's trade 'card' (right) includes vignettes of the wooden hand press and of the rolling press for engraved jobbing on which both these examples were performed.

The KING *and* QUEENE *conjoyned,*
The Kentish news related,
Our Forces are united,
A publique Fast appointed.

Numb. 8

Mercurius Civicus.
LONDONS
INTELLIGENCER·
OR,
Truth impartially related from thence
to the whole Kingdome, to
prevent mif-information.

From *Thurſday, Iuly* 13. to *Thurſday. July* 20. 1643.

Hereas it is the generall expeƈtation and defire of moſt
people to be informed of the true ſtate of the Army under the command of his Excellency the Parliaments
Lord Generall; It will not therefore be amiſſe in the
firſt place to impart ſomething of the late intelligence
from thence, which was informed by Letters from
Steny-ſtratford, tv this effeƈt, That on Saturday laſt, being the 15 of

H *Iuly*

Fig. 31. Page size $7\frac{3}{8} \times 5\frac{3}{4}$ in.

the title—a typographical innovation still used, though today it is usually on the right-hand side of the masthead.

Not long after this enterprising issue *Mercurius Civicus* included an illustration in the text. The block had been used once before, on the front page where it was not explained. Yet it was top news: a novel weapon, and quaint though it looks to modern eyes, apparently most effective for bashing the Roundheads. The block had been specially cut and could not have been used on other occasions, like the fires and the scaffold scenes of earlier days, nor, since the illustration was embedded in the text, could separate sheets have been sold. The publishers of *Mercurius Civicus* understood that the expense of cutting a block to be used

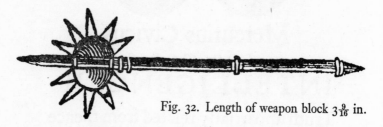

Fig. 32. Length of weapon block $3\frac{9}{16}$ in.

only twice was outweighed by the interest it created for their paper. Their venture was not to be regularly imitated for more than two hundred years.

It was the newspapers and the freedom with which they commented on politics that drove the Government, supported for other reasons by the Stationers' Company, to lay more and more restrictions upon the printing trade, and in September 1655 Cromwell, then Lord Protector, suppressed all newspapers except for two official sheets, one published on Thursdays, the other on Mondays. They contained sixteen pages, and the price of advertisements went up to 2/6 an insertion. This situation, with only two licensed periodicals, continued after the Restoration, when one was the *London Gazette*, founded in November 1665 and still in existence today. The *Gazette* showed a further increase in page size: $12\frac{1}{2}$ by 7 inches.[21]

There were, however, spasmodic clandestine publications. The struggle of the Whigs to exclude the Catholic Duke of York, Charles II's brother and heir, from the throne, together with a lapse in the Printing Act between 1679 and 1683, resulted in an

The Athenian Mercury:

Resolving WEEKLY all the most

Nice and Curious Questions

Propos'd by the INGENIOUS.

Tuesday, March, 31st. 1690.

THose who are concerned in this *Paper*, hope it may be imputed to *Modesty*, rather than *Weakness*, that they are still forced to make further Explanations of their Design; they own it had been more cautiously expressed, if the *Promise* had been to endeavour the Answering of all lawful Questions, rather than absolutely performed it, tho' every Ingenious Reader will make such an interpretation.——

We find the Questions grow so fast upon us, among which are several *Duplicates* with *Complaints* of their not being yet answered; that to obviate the Confusion which thence may follow, we intend to Publish our *Paper* twice a Week, viz. every *Tuesday* and *Saturday*. And in the mean time, till we are got clear of those already on our hands, we desire the *Curious Inquirers* to reserve their *New Questions*, till we shall give publick *Advertisement* that we have dispatcht all the *Old* ones, at least such as deserve an *Answer*.

Quest. 1. *Why Mr. Smith the Coffee-Man in your Advertisements, and plain Matthew and Luke in your Quotations?*

Answ. The first to comply with a *Civil Custom*, the last for the same reason, as some of the greatest *Divines* of the *Establisht* Church, do the same both in their *Sermons* and *Writings*, either through *inadvertency*, or because 'tis matter of so small *Consequence*, that 'tis hardly worth taking notice of; but however, rather than that should breed a *Quarrel*, or we be taken for *Quakers*, from our *Aversion* to any such *slight Garniture*, we'll take care for the future to mend this *matter*, and it shall be *Holy St. Matthew*, and *Blessed St. Luke* in our next Quotation.

Quest. 2. *What causes the Ebbing and Flowing of the Sea?*

Answ. *Aristotle* (if we may believe what *Celius Rhodiginus* says lib. 29. *Antiquarum Lectionum Cap.* 8.) died for Grief because he could not understand the reason of it, which he need not have done if he had asked himself the Question: What is the Reason of the Sea Motion? Which is nothing else but the necessary Law of Creation, or the first Establisht Order of Nature. An Order, without which the whole Fabrick had revolved into its first Chaos, for had the Sun been fixt in any one Part of the Element, the opposite part of the Earth had been burnt up, and all the rest froze, and Consequently all the Terraqueal Globe incapacitated for fructification and Generation: In like manner, if the main Ocean had had no particular Commission or Order from its Creator (which is the only Efficient Cause for a Flux and Reflux, it would have Stagnated and Corrupted, and by consequence unfit for Procreation of Fishes, and Navigation. If it be asked why the *Mediterranean*, *West-Indian* and *Caspian* Seas, and the *Mare-del-Zur* Seas have not their Tide? We answer, That the *Mediterranean* and *West-Indian* Seas, have their Motions, and empty

Subterranean Passages into the *Chinese* or other Seas, as does our *Canal* in *St. James's Park*. The *Magellanick* runs with so great a rapidity into the *Mare del Zur*, That no Wind nor Art can force a ship up it, which *Motion* serves instead of a Flux, and Reflux, and diverts the Inconveniences aforesaid.

Quest. 3. *What's the reason that some Men have no Beards?*

Answ. A want of heat and a due disposition of Nature: So where there is not heat enough to open the Pores, for the Excrescency of Hair, that *Humidity* and *Moisture* which is the natural *Cause* of Hair, retires to other parts of the Body, more adapt and better prepared for Expulsion.

Quest. 5. *Whence proceeds weeping and laughing for the same Cause?*

Answ. 'Tis from an unequal Compressure of the *Muscles*, by the Passions: as for Instance, touch a place of your Body and it itches, rub the same place hard and it smarts: In like manner when the Passions act easily upon the *Muscles*, a smile ensues, if a little harder it causes laughter; if harder, it causes laughing and Crying at the same time; but if it be very violent, it causes only crying.

Quest. 6. *Whether there be Witches? and what good Books have been written on that Subject?*

Answ. I answer, there are *Witches*, unless we can suppose both God and Man would conspire to deceive us; the good Books written on that *Subject*, are the *Holy Bible* and the *Histories of all Nations*.

To be more explicite; by *Witches* we mean such as act beyond the *ordinary Power of Nature*, by the help of *Wicked Spirits*: The Proof whereof being matter of *Fact*, must rely wholly on the *Credibility* of *Witnesses*; God's Authority is unquestionable: That *God has suffered a Witch to live*: and such a Witch as the definition supposes, for such they were whom *Saul* destroyed according to this Law, one of whom was that at *Endor*, whose Story we have 1 *Sam.* 28. *Saul* desired her to *Divine*, and bring up whom he should name, that by the help of Wicked Spirits. By the *Familiar Spirit*, 'tis true the *Webiterians* pretend the Words were well translated. The Word *Ob* which I think is here used, (for I have the Original by me) they tell us signifies only a sort of *Bottle*, or some such ridiculous thing in which the Conjurer mutter with a squeaking Voice to cheat those who come to him: at which rate all our *Puppet-Players* must be hanged for Conjurers: they must make *God* unjust to punish with Death a Cheat or Sleight of Hand, or shift in Nature, whereinto they resolve all *Witchcraft*: *Saul* also and his Courtiers were the most stupid of Men' being so grossly imposed on, and all Mankind are Knaves or Fools, and they themselves only Wise and Honest.

As for *Humane Testimonies*, this matter has all the *Requisites of Credibility* that any thing is capable of: 'tis affirmed by most Men, prudent Men, good Men, who had no Interest nor Temptation to impose: All the World in a matter which demanded not one jot of prudence, but whereof they were competent Judges, in all Places, Countries and Ages, hardly any History e're written but giving some Instances, agreeing still in the main, both in *Africa*, *Asia*, *Europe* and *America*: To disbelieve it were to arraign the Justice of our fore-Fathers, and Wisdom of their Laws, who according to their acknowledged hanged up a Parcel of foolish Old Women, merely because they had cracked their Brains, and lost their Senses: In a word, a Man may as modestly affirm, there is no such place as *Rome*; no, no such thing as

Fig. 33. Page size 12½ × 7 in.

outburst of violent and embittered propaganda for the Protestant cause. The medium was the periodical press. The numerous publications were not newspapers, for they seldom contained news: they were attacks animated by the discovery by Titus Oates and his friends of the 'Popish Plot'.[22] One hesitates to call these productions essay papers. 'Essay' is a mild word, and hardly conveys the vigour and coarseness of many of the writers, both Protestant and Catholic. They make the journalists of the Civil War period, who were not mealy-mouthed when they abused political opponents, read as primly as a schoolgirls' magazine. Vigour and coarseness are elements peculiarly successful in periodical publications, as modern publishers well know.

In the less embittered atmosphere after the Revolution of 1688 and the accession of William III and his consort, several publications were founded that were not newspapers and which approach more closely to our concept of a magazine. The *Athenian Mercury* was among the first, founded in March 1690. In that it had no diversity of contents, we would not call it, strictly, a magazine. The publisher produced a question-and-answer paper, a device already exploited by the propagandists of the previous reign. The Athenian Society, a most learned body, were prepared to answer such vexed questions as where swallows go in the winter or that very vexed question, whether women have souls. The publisher, John Dunton, was himself the Athenian Society: he later confessed that the first meeting of that learned body was held in his own brain. Both question and answer were printed in full on a single sheet, size $12\frac{1}{2}$ by 7 inches, like the contemporary newspaper, and with newspaper layout. The *Athenian Mercury* appeared twice weekly and cost one penny.

The success of this publication encouraged the Ladies Society to embark on the *Ladies Mercury*. No doubt the society was composed entirely of men, but they promised to answer all questions relating to 'love etc . . . with the zeal and softness becoming the sex'. The same questions are still being answered in correspondence columns today.

There were other formulae. The *London Mercury*, similar in format to its contemporaries, contained a single essay, and in other papers like the *Observator* the dialogue was used. There is an overall variety, but not within the limits of a single publication.

So we come to the *Collection for Improvement of Husbandry and*

A
COLLECTION
For Improvement of
Husbandry and Trade.

Friday, May 18. 1694.

To fatten Capons, and prepare Hoggs for Pease. Beer made with Bran. 'Tis used by Brewers and Dyers. And for cleansing Pewter. And for Horses and Cows. The making of Starch. Sometimes damaged Corn used instead of Bran. A way to make Rusty Wire bright. A brave way to fat Hogs. How Measling and Scabbiness in Hogs are cured. Hog's Dung. Price of Corn, &c. in many Counties. Price of English Commodities in London. Price of Actions in Companies. Price of Cloth, &c. An Abstract of the Bills of Mortality, &c.

TO make a perfect History every thing must be taken in; and now comes *Bran*, which is used in a great many cases for *Horses, Hogs,* and *Poultry.*

Make *Cakes* with Bran and Water, bake them pretty hard, and then feed Capons with them, either dry or steep't in Water, 'twill make them fatten bravely and quick.

Boil'd Bran milk-warm clothes Hogs, and is a brave preparative if so given some Weeks before they eat Pease.

I am told that if you take a Bushel and half of good *Wheat Bran,* with a Gallon of *Molasses,* and some *Ginger,* 'twill with Liquor (*Water*) make a Barrel of very good Table-beer.

And Bran is often used to cover the Liquor in Brewing, and in the Mash tub. The Dyers also use it.

Another great use of Bran is to wash Dishes with, especially in the Country where they keep Hogs; for the Bran cleans the Dishes, and takes up the Fat for the nourishment of them.

And scalded Bran is often given to Horses and Cows.

The manner of making *Starch* is as follows:

They take Twenty Quarters of Bran (but when Corn grows Musty, or by accident is Wet and sticks to the side of the Bags, or has any other disaster, (except growing) they use it as buying it cheaper, and having more flower in it) this is shot into a Vat, and then Water is pumpt into it as much as is sufficient, and there it stands sometimes a Fortnight, in which time at first all the Meal or Bran rises; but when it is well soak't, it sinks to the bottom, and the Liquor will grow very sowre, and so much, that 'tis usual with the Pin-makers to bring their rusty Brass Wire which looks very Black, to be put into some of it, which in a little time will fetch off all the Rust, and make it look as bright as it is desired Brass should do. In the management of this, 'tis strained through a course sieve, and afterwards a very fine Sieve, that no Clods may be there, nor Bran; after which it settles, and the Water being drained out, the sediment is cut into

square Pieces, Eight, Ten, or Twelve Inches thick, and laid to dry in the Air; and when pretty well so, 'tis put into a Stove to be dried more; and when enough, 'tis taken out in whole pieces; but if broken, it will separate into innumerable pieces like Pillars, and be very White, as you may see in what they call *White Starch.*

The bottom parts will be sour and Whiter than the top, and of that Bottom is made the White Starch, and is the fine Flower, as I told you in *Numb.* 89. The Top is courser, and is usually sold to make Paste with for such as use Paste instead of Glue.

The Bran that is separated, with Wash, (*Stiller's Wash* if they can get it) feeds Hogs, and these are kept a great many together in Huts boarded at bottom and top with a declivity that all their filth may run towards the Front, before which is a Fence of Boards, and under that the Troughs for their Food: Some Pails of Water thrown into the Huts will wash them clean, and by help of a Broom they may easily be kept clean by this means.

I have seen the Hogs look almost as White as Pigs, and they fatten and thrive bravely.

If the Hogs be foul and Measled, by giving them some of the Sour Liquor it will cure them, and cause them to throw it quite off.

The Dung of these Hogs is reckoned good for nothing, because, as the Starch men say, they cause abundance of Weeds to grow; but methinks it will make Weeds grow, it may easily be appropriated to some better purposes.

Next *Friday* expect more,

From Yours, &c.

John Houghton, F. R. S.

S. Bartholomew-Lane, behind the
Royal-Exchange, London.

Fig. 34. Page size 13¼×7½ in.

Trade, founded in March 1691. The title is ponderous; but significant. That word 'Collection' is an attempt to express the unfamiliar notion of variety of contents, a notion for which today we use the word 'magazine'. The publisher himself wrote a main article in each issue, always a sensible piece on a subject such as brick-making, stocks and shares, the nature of soils or of precious stones, and he occasionally appealed to women readers by including recipes. Other regular contents included an abstract of the bills of mortality, the weather forecast and commodity prices. The *Collection* was so successful an idea that a second sheet was filled with advertisements and eventually editorial labours were abandoned.

The true ancestor of our modern magazines was the *Gentleman's Journal*, a monthly miscellany of wide range: news, history, poetry, translations, short stories—called 'novels'—and eight pages of music. The result filled forty-eight pages, and the publishers found it convenient to revert to the dimensions of the newsbook. Owing to its character and size an editor (Peter Motteux) was required, as well as contributors, who included Dryden and Purcell; and the appearance of these figures marks another stage in the development of the periodical press.

The *Athenian Mercury*, the *Collection* and the *Gentleman's Journal* all belong to that section of the periodical press that is not concerned with news. It is not easy to find a single comprehensive term for these productions that are not newspapers. Loosely, they may be described as magazines; but very loosely. Their contents are varied, like those of the *Collection* and the *Gentleman's Journal*, and if they do contain news, as the *Gentleman's Journal* did, they do so as a record. This class of publication, the alternative to newspapers, is today of huge variety and vast total circulation. At the end of the seventeenth century, it had only been invented, but with the lifting of restrictions on the printing trade its development in London was accelerated.

NOTES

1 Stanley Morison in *Venice and the Arabesque* (Privately printed, 1955, copy at St Bride's) gives some account of the early casting of type ornament.

2 The *Trewe Encounter* was found in a binding (Inc. 3213.5) at the University Library, Cambridge.

3 The University Library, Cambridge, has four pages of the Marsh newsbook. There is only the title-page in Bagford (Harl. MSS., 5919, no. 242).

4 Cecil Papers at Hatfield House (microfilm at B.M.), xxx, 60, contains a series dated 1575.

5 Mr Stanley Morison has a small collection of manuscript newsletters to which he referred in *The Origins of the Newspaper* (Privately printed, 1954, copy at St Bride's).

6 P. M. Handover, *The Second Cecil* (London, 1959) contains an account of Cecil's intelligence service.

7 D. C. Collins, *A Handlist of News Pamphlets, 1590-1610* (London, 1943). Copies of many newsbooks listed by Mr Collins as only held at Peterborough are now in the B.M. (C. 132.h.25).

8 There is an amusing block of a flood, used twice early in 1607 for floods in Somerset, Norfolk and other places, again within a week by another printer for floods in South Wales and also for a fourth occasion (S.T.C. 22915, 22916, 18021, 10011).

9 Harry H. Hoppe, 'John Wolfe, Printer and Publisher', *The Library* (1933-4), xiv, 241. Wolfe was not presented, as one would expect, at the end of his apprenticeship. Either he did not complete it or he preferred to attach himself to the Fishmongers, a more powerful Company.

10 See Arber, ii, 514 ff. and i, 549. Publications purporting to describe the Armada of 1588 are fakes; as are those of the Gunpowder Plot, which was not 'reported'.

11 Arber, ii, 588 (July 5, 1591) and 597 (October 23, 1591).

12 There is an account of Barnes and Phelippes in P. M. Handover, *op. cit.*

13 B.M., C. 132. h. 25 is a collection of Wolfe's newsbooks and contains the letter signed T.B. and those 'Published by authority'.

14 The map illustrated 'A True Discourse of the Most Happy Victories Obtained by the French King', found in the B.M. collection *op. cit.* The leaf appears to be signature A1 and would, therefore, be the outside leaf.

15 The Introduction to *The Times Handlist* is out of date and should be used cautiously.

16 F. Dahl, *Bibliography of English Corantos and Periodical News-books 1620-42* (London, 1952), believes the N.B. stood for Nathaniel Butter. Other authorities are Stanley Morison, and S. H. Steinberg, *Five Hundred Years of Printing* (London, 1959).

17 Leona Rostenberg, 'Nathaniel Butter and Nicholas Bourne, First "Masters of the Staple" ', *The Library* (March 1957), xii, 23, gives an excellent account of the two booksellers and news publishers.

18 These newsbooks are Burney 2. The Burney Collection at the B.M. contains all the periodicals hereafter mentioned.

19 These entries are in Arber, ii, pp. 79 and 93 ff.

20 Stanley Morison, *The English Newspaper* (Cambridge, 1932), is lavishly illustrated from the Burney Collection.

21 J. B. Williams, *A History of English Journalism to the Foundation of the Gazette* (London, 1908), is particularly good on early advertising.

22 For example, from Burney 81, *The Weekly Discoverer Stripp'd Naked: or Jest and Earnest Exposed to Public View in his Proper Colours* (1681) or *The Weekly Visions of the Late Popish Plot* (1681).

V

The Periodical Press in the Eighteenth Century

RELUCTANCE to enforce the Printing Act after 1691 encouraged the appearance of several weekly or bi-weekly literary papers in that year. The news publishers, being more vulnerable, were more cautious: they waited until their right to appear was incontestable, and only after May 1695 was there a florescence of newspapers.

Thrice weekly now became the normal interval between issues, since proprietors in London depended for distribution upon the posts from abroad and from the provinces which arrived in London three times a week. These posts were of great importance in the development of the periodical press, and many of the new journals acknowledged their obligation by including the word POST in the title, alongside an ornamental block of the post-boy or postman galloping across the country, blowing his horn, such as had been used in earlier German newspapers. Examples include the *London Post*, the *Flying Post*, the *Old Post-Master*, the *Post Boy* and the *Post-Man*. The blocks in the masthead were still the only illustrations in the newspaper (see Plate X).[1]

When the *London Gazette* went to $12\frac{1}{2}$ by 7 inches, two other changes were made: the type size of the text matter was decreased and the text was set in two columns, since to have set to the full measure would have given an unwieldy line. Thus, the pre-1695 *Gazette* had contained an unusual amount of reading matter. The developments were adopted by the various *Posts* and the paper size underwent another slight increase, to $13\frac{1}{2}$ or 14 by $7\frac{1}{2}$ inches.[2]

Since the *Gazette* did not change it began to look old-fashioned, but occasionally a second sheet was included in an issue. Then

the price 2d was added after the imprint—never at the top of page 1, where we expect to find it today. Other newspapers did not announce their price, possibly because the habit of subscription was general, casual sales being made by the proprietor's own agents, usually women and still known as Mercury women, although boys were beginning to be used.

Evening newspapers, thrice weekly, were also established after 1696, some of them being daily newspapers published late. *Dawks' Newsletter* was the first evening, and the *Evening Post* (August 1706) the first to include the word in the title. As yet there were no Sunday newspapers.[3]

With all this activity of creation among the printed newspapers it was natural that there should be a decline, the decline of the handwritten newsletter. Throughout the seventeenth century it had flourished. For most of the period the manuscript newsletter had been the only source of home news and the only source of any news that appeared thrice weekly. Some years ago a collection from the last years of the century was sold at Messrs Hodgson, Chancery Lane, for several thousand pounds. The manuscript newsletter did not have to be licensed and L'Estrange never managed to secure control over its appearance. But the value of these letters as source material for historians has been little recognized in this country.[4] The practice survived into the second half of the eighteenth century, chiefly as a vehicle of rather spiced political gossip.

The format of such letters was the same as it had been in the sixteenth century, a folio or quarto sheet folded to make four or more pages, the last being left blank for the address, and the contraction 'Sr', which had become the usual opening, was sometimes set out decoratively. This format and decoration were imitated by Ichabod Dawks in his handsome *Newsletter*, founded in 1696, which had a successful life of twenty years—remarkable at the time. He even procured a fine script type to complete the imitation of the manuscript sheet. This publication is an instance of the typographical conservatism of newspaper readers, who like their newspapers to look familiar, even a little outmoded. In the pages of magazines, on the other hand, and even on feature pages of modern newspapers, the typography can be more bold and novel.

Dawks was an extreme example of the specialization in

equipment that was beginning to divide the periodical printers from the book printers. This tendency was not as pronounced at the end of the seventeenth century as it became a hundred years later. Nevertheless, certain printers were able to specialize in periodical publishing. They stocked themselves with the sizes of type used in newspapers, and they had to have adequate stocks since duplicate setting was often necessary. Their presses, too, were modified in order to take larger sheets of paper and to be worked as easily as possible by the pressmen. There is at St Bride's Institute in the City an eighteenth-century newspaper press with an unusually large platen and a specially prepared frisket. The mechanism also differs slightly from the seventeenth-century book press.

We now come to a date of the utmost importance: March 11, 1702. On this day, a Wednesday, Samuel Buckley published the first daily newspaper, the *Daily Courant*. Here was a triumph for the notion of periodicity. Butter and Bourne had managed to publish as often as four times a week, but not regularly and not on fixed days. The periodicity of the thrice-weeklies founded after 1695 was forced on them by the periodicity of the country posts, upon which they depended for distribution outside London. But Buckley in his *Daily Courant* was concerned with the maximum periodicity in news publishing, the means of distribution being subsidiary.

The *Daily Courant* was a single sheet like its contemporaries, slightly shorter in page depth, $12\frac{1}{2}$ by $7\frac{1}{2}$ inches, and at first the supply of news was so scanty that only one side of the paper was filled. There was no editorial comment: the author (or compiler) stated that it might be supposed people had 'sense enough to make reflections for themselves'—a supposition no modern newspaper proprietor would care to make.

There is no doubt that reflections were being made. The *Daily Courant* was founded because the foreign news had become of overwhelming importance, so that a day-to-day report could find a ready circulation. This was the period of the Continental wars in which Marlborough was to add so gloriously to the reputation of British arms. It is significant that the *Daily Courant* began publication in March when the year's campaign opened after the inactivity of the winter, and it was not long before the columns could be filled with news.

The Daily Courant.

Wednesday, March 11. 1702.

From the Harlem Courant, Dated March 18. N. S.

Naples, Feb. 22.

ON Wednesday last, our New Viceroy, the Duke of Escalona, arriv'd here with a Squadron of the Galleys of Sicily. He made his Entrance drest in a French habit ; and to give us the greater Hopes of the King's coming hither, went to Lodge in one of the little Palaces, leaving the Royal one for his Majesty. The Marquis of Grigni is also arriv'd here with a Regiment of French.

Rome, Feb. 25. In a Military Congregation of State that was held here, it was Resolv'd to draw a Line from Ascoli to the Borders of the Ecclesiastical State, thereby to hinder the Incursions of the Transalpine Troops. Orders are sent to Civita Vecchia to fit out the Galleys, and to strengthen the Garrison of that Place. Signior Casali is made Governor of Perugia. The Marquis del Vasto, and the Prince de Caserta continue still in the Imperial Embassador's Palace ; where his Excellency has a Guard of 50 Men every Night in Arms. The King of Portugal has desir'd the Arch-Bishoprick of Lisbon, vacant by the Death of Cardinal Sousa, for the Infante his second Son, who is about 11 Years old.

Vienna, Mar. 4. Orders are sent to the 4 Regiments of Foot, the 2 of Cuirassiers, and to that of Dragoons, which are broke up from Hungary, and are on their way to Italy, and which consist of about 14 or 15000 Men, to hasten their March thither with all Expedition. The 6 new Regiments of Hussars that are now raising, are in so great a forwardness, that they will be compleat, and in a Condition to march by the middle of May. Prince Lewis of Baden has written to Court, to excuse himself from coming thither, his Presence being so very necessary, and so much desir'd on the Upper-Rhine.

Franckfort, Mar. 12. The Marquiss d' Uxelles is come to Strasburg, and is to draw together a Body of some Regiments of Horse and Foot from the Garisons of Alsace ; but will not lessen those of Strasburg and Landau, which are already very weak. On the other hand, the Troops of His Imperial Majesty, and his Allies, are going to form a Body near Germesheim in the Palatinate, of which Place, as well as of the Lines at Spires, Prince Lewis of Baden is expected to take a View, in three or four days. The English and Dutch Ministers, the Count of Frise, and the Baron Vander Meer, and likewise the Imperial Envoy Count Lowenstein, are gone to Nordlingen, and it is hop'd that in a short time we shall hear from thence of some favourable Resolutions for the Security of the Empire.

Liege, Mar. 14. The French have taken the Cannon de Longie, who was Secretary to the Dean de Mean, out of our Castle, where he has been for some time a Prisoner; and have deliver'd him to the Provost of Maubeuge, who has carry'd him from hence, but we do not know whither.

Paris, Mar. 13. Our Letters from Italy say, That most of our Reinforcements were Landed there ; that the Imperial and Ecclesiastical Troops seem to live very peaceably with one another in the Country of Parma, and that the Duke of Vendome, as he was visiting several Posts, was within 100 Paces of falling into the Hands of the Germans. The Duke of Chartres, the Prince of Conti, and several other Princes of the Blood, are to make the Campaign in

Flanders under the Duke of Burgundy ; and the Duke of Maine is to Command upon the Rhine.

From the Amsterdam Courant, Dated Mar. 18.

Rome, Feb. 25. We are taking here all possible Precautions for the Security of the Ecclesiastical State in this present Conjuncture, and have desir'd to raise 3000 Men in the Cantons of Switzerland. The Pope has appointed the Duke of Berwick to be his Lieutenant-General, and he is to Command 6000 Men on the Frontiers of Naples : He has also settled upon him a Pension of 6000 Crowns a year during Life.

From the Paris Gazette, Dated Mar. 18. 1702.

Naples, Febr. 17. 600 French Soldiers are arrived here, and are expected to be follow'd by 3400 more. A Courier that came hither on the 14th. has brought Letters by which we are assur'd that the King of Spain designs to be here towards the end of March ; and accordingly Orders are given to make the necessary Preparations against his Arrival. The two Troops of Horse that were Commanded to the Abruzzo are posted at Pescara with a Body of Spanish Foot, and others in the Fort of Montorio.

Paris, March. 18. We have Advice from Toulon of the 5th instant, that the Wind having long stood favourable, 22000 Men were already sail'd for Italy, that 2500 more were Embarking, and that by the 15th it was hoped they might all get thither. The Count d' Estrees arriv'd there on the Third instant, and set all hands at work to fit out the Squadron of 9 Men of War and some Fregats, that are appointed to carry the King of Spain to Naples. His Catholick Majesty will go on Board the *Thunderer*, of 110 Guns.

We have Advice by an Express from Rome of the 18th of February, That notwithstanding the pressing Instances of the Imperial Embassadour, the Pope had Condemn'd the Marquis del Vasto to lose his Head and his Estate to be confiscated, for not appearing to Answer the Charge against him of Publickly Scandalizing Cardinal Janson.

ADVERTISEMENT.

IT will be found from the Foreign Prints, which from time to time, as Occasion offers, will be mention'd in this Paper, that the Author has taken Care to be duly furnish'd with all that comes from Abroad in any Language. And for an Assurance that he will not, under Pretence of having Private Intelligence, impose any Additions of feign'd Circumstances to an Action, but give his Extracts fairly and Impartially ; at the beginning of each Article he will quote the Foreign Paper from whence 'tis taken, that the Publick, seeing from what Country a piece of News comes with the Allowance of that Government, may be better able to Judge of the Credibility and Fairness of the Relation : Nor will he take upon him to give any Comments or Conjectures of his own, but will relate only Matter of Fact ; supposing other People to have Sense enough to make Reflections for themselves.

This Courant (as the Title shews) will be Publish'd Daily : being design'd to give all the Material News as soon as every Post arrives : and is confin'd to half the Compass, to save the Publick at least half the Impertinences, of ordinary News-Papers.

LONDON. Sold by E. *Mallet*, next Door to the *King's-Arms* Tavern at *Fleet-Bridge.*

Fig. 35. Page size 13¼×7 in. The top right-hand corner of this Burney copy is mutilated. (March 11 in England was March 22 on the Continent.)

But for the readers of the time there was more to the news than the progress of a campaign. The war itself was a party matter—the adjective was then new that has since become inseparable from government in this country—and just as religious differences had once dominated national life, and prayer books and sermons had dominated publishing, so now it was the turn of politics, and of political tracts and newspapers.

It is desirable for newspaper publishers that their readers should be interested in politics, which change day by day, rather than in religion which is hardly diurnal. In the early eighteenth century there was also a second factor, the commercial expansion of this country, a circumstance which demanded the frequent publication of news of changing conditions of trade. In Queen Anne's reign, the military campaigns had their part to play in the development of the newspaper press, and important also was the emergence of a settled, rich and closely knit society. It was satisfactory to the news publishers that the news in one issue should be discussed in the coffee-houses; it encouraged the sale of the next issue. It was satisfactory that people began to prefer the *Flying Post* or the *Post Boy* or the *Daily Courant*; the competition was healthy and served to strengthen the periodical press as a whole.

The new society that was demanding plays and poems and such light reading matter created new periodicals of entertainment. At the beginning of the eighteenth century these were numerous. The intention of a title such as the *Diverting Post* is plain, and this sheet, founded in 1704, may be classed as a magazine for it contained varied contents: a quantity of poetry set in small italic —and how tiresome it is to read—theatrical and social news, music, short poems, riddles and songs. The riddles became a main diversion and readers were encouraged to contribute, a practice often adopted by periodical proprietors, who thus learn a considerable amount about their readers besides filling space cheaply. In appearance the *Diverting Post* exactly resembled its newspaper contemporaries, but since it was a single sheet published monthly, the price of sixpence was high.

The *Humours of a Coffee-House* and its successor the *Weekly Comedy* were dialogue papers that exactly reflected the social *milieu* where they were read. They contained four pages, the size of the Puritan newspapers of the Civil War period, which

I

(65)   Numb. XVII.

THE
Weekly Comedy:
OR, THE
Humours of the AGE:
As Daily Acted in
Town and Country.

To be Continued every Friday.

Dramatis Personæ.

Levy, *a Recruiting Officer.*	Venture, *a Merchant.*	Double, *a Time-ferver.*
Hazard, *a Gamefter.*	Talley, *a Stock-Jobber.*	Bays, *a Poet.*
Bite, *a Sharper.*	Querpo, *a Quack.*	Log, *a Mariner.*
Prim, *a Beau.*	Trick, *a Lawyer.*	Harlem, *a News-writer.*
Blunt, *a Plain-Dealer.*	Grim, *an Aftrologer.*	Guzzle, *a Hard Drinker.*
Whim, *a Projector.*	Froth, *a Punfter.*	Bohee, *the Coffee-man.*

Note, That we shall change our Scene from Place to Place, and vary our
Characters as Occasion shall require.

Friday December the 5th, 1707.

SCENE *a Tavern continu'd.* Bays, Double, Venture, *and* Harlem *at a Table.*

Bays. WELL, Gentlemen, since I have ventured to throw some of my Poetical Excrements under your Noses, pray be so kind as to tell me how they favour with you?

Double. They smell a little too rank of *High-Church,* for my Noftrils. I am

for *Moderation* in all things, but that's a Vertue you Poets have seldom any regard to.

Venture. I confefs that Deform'd Off-Spring that you feem to be fo Fond of, was firft Calved into the World by your Party. But no fooner was the *Illegitimate Issue* Born and Chriften'd,
R   but

Fig. 36. Page size 8¾×6 in.

made them look very small against contemporaries. The change of format had the effect of distinguishing the *Weekly Comedy* from other periodicals of entertainment and one is inclined to believe that it was adopted for this reason (see Fig 36). There was enterprise among those who owned it, for they drew attention to the serial nature of the dialogue: 'to be continued every Friday'.

The question-and-answer device continued to be popular. Defoe once announced in his political *Review* that he would answer questions and was so swamped with replies that special supplements had to be run off to accommodate them; but the frivolity of many of the questions made Defoe impatient, and he abandoned the idea. Others exploited it, accepted all the host of questions on manners, taste, etiquette and the conduct of love affairs that were asked by a society anxious to be 'polite'.

The *British Apollo* was a typical example, four pages, one devoted to poetry.[5] Most surprising, perhaps, is the number of religious questions, usually seeking very precise information. For example, several people wanted to know the age of our Lord when he was crucified. The illustration chosen (Fig 37) shows the variety: an arithmetical problem, a question about Hebrew, and one of those steady favourites on women—will they be resurrected? (The answer was comforting.)

Advertisements were plentiful. They reveal how often watches were stolen at this period, though *British Apollo* readers do seem to have suffered more in this respect than other citizens. In every issue there are two or three insertions for 'lost'—which must be a euphemism—gold squeezing watches, presumably what we would call a hunter, with a hinged lid. Servants, too, ran away with distressing frequency, but in this respect the readers of the *British Apollo* were no less afflicted than readers of other journals.

A bi-weekly, Wednesdays and Fridays, the *British Apollo* was obtained by subscription, 2s at the end of each quarter, and each number was delivered to the subscriber's house by boys, who had their 'walks', not 'rounds'. The proprietors eventually saw the need to make the *Apollo* tri-weekly, for customers, and particularly the coffee-house keepers, were taking in some other publication to provide reading matter on Mondays.

The proprietors were aware of the value of ancillary publications: indexes, title-pages and lists of contents for the bound volumes, folders for single copies, back numbers and abridgements, all were advertised. When the public complained that the title-page, price 1d, cost as much as an issue, the proprietors quickly explained that although it contained so few words it cost as much to print; but the addition of a preface satisfied the grumblers. Sets were available with the exhortation, familiar to us, that numbers were limited and application should be made at once—of course, the sets were still available a year or so later.

One publicity gambit was the *British Apollo* concert—an enterprise on the principle of Northcliffe's great exhibitions at Olympia. Unfortunately, the *Apollo* had not worked out the economics. At first, it was proposed to publish in each issue music eventually to be performed at a concert organized for readers. There were initial difficulties, not the least of which was the printer's failure to obtain the music types in time. Then, it was found not enough to

The British Apollo;

OR,

Curious Amusements for the INGENIOUS.

To which are added the moſt

Material Occurrences Foreign and Domeſtick.

Perform'd by a Society of GENTLEMEN.

From **Friday** May 21th. to **Wedneſday** May 26th. 1708.

Whereas this Paper now, beſides the greet Numbers taken in, at Publick-Houses; is taken in at many more Private-Houses than any other Paper, and by Conſequence likely to be of more Effect for Advertiſements than any others; alſo our taking Care that nothing ſhall be taken in but what is Creditable, otherwiſe we might have much ſlit'd the Paper before this time; we impeaſe it may be of Incouragement to People to Advertiſe in this Paper.

Any Perſons, upon directing their Letters to the Printer ſuperſcrib'd, for the *British Apollo*; may have this Paper brought to their Houſes at two Shillings a Quarter, by the Men who carry them, thoſe who come in within the Quarter, to have proportionable Deductions at the End: Alſo the Monthly Papers for *April* and *May*: Likewiſe the Books of Guards neatly bound to keep 'em in, at two Shillings a piece. It is deſired all Letters with Queſtions be directed thither, or to Mr. *Keble* in *Weſt-minſter-Hall*, or to Mr. *Bickerton*, at the Golden *Flower-de-luce*, in St. *Paul's-Church-Yard*, Bookſellers: Where whole Sets may be had from the Beginning; at which Places likewiſe, Advertiſements are taken in: But all who deſire Sets, and to have them conſtantly deliver'd at their Houſes, muſt direct their Letters as above. *Note*, that they who have whole Sets are only to pay a Shilling for the 12 before Lady-Day, and the reſt to go on this Quarter.

Q. *Pray Demonſtrate that Rule in Specious Arithmetick, that to take away an Affirmative Quantity, is to add a Negative, and to &c?*

A. An Affirmative Quantity denotes the Poſſeſſion of ſuch a Sum, but a Negative Quantity implies the abſence of it, or a Debt of ſuch a value. As therefore, when *From* my Poſſeſſion of 100 *l.* the Poſſeſſion of 60 *l.* is taken away, I am then worth 40 *l.* So, when by my Poſſeſſion of 100 *l.* is added a Debt, which I muſt pay, of 60 *l.* I am then worth the ſame 40 *l.*

Q. *Doctor* Heylin *poſitive'y ſays, the Hebrew was not the Primitive Language?* Coſmography, Pag. 15. Line 1.

A. If you read the Paſſage a ſecond time, you will find, that, while ſpeaking o' the Language, that was uſ'd in common before the Confuſion of Languages, he uſes ſome ſuch Expreſſion, *Whether it were the Hebrew or any other Language*, which ſure can reach no further than a doubt. But what he poſitively aſſerts, is only this, that the *Hebrew* Language was not, as the *Jews* contend, incommunicably confin'd to the Family of *Heber*, and therefore the Paſſage, which you miſtake, does no way hin-

der our concluding from the unmingled Purity and ſignificant Etymologies of it's Words, that the *Hebrew* was the Primitive Language.

Q. *How are thoſe Expreſſions of our Saviour's to be underſtood?* You will not come unto me, that you may have Life; *and An another Place?* No man can come unto me, except my Father draw him.

A. The ſeeming Contrariety of ſuch Expreſſions evidently ſhews, that, as We can do nothing of our ſelves without God's Aſſiſtance, ſo we cannot expect, that He ſhou'd work in us without our own Concurrence.

Q. *A Promiſe being made to* Abraham *of a Son, as we read* Gen. 17, 17. *he fell on his Face and laugh'd. The like Promiſe being made to* Sarah, *as we read in* Gen. 18, 12. *She laughed too. But* Sarah *is reproved, and* Abraham *applauded. Now I deſire to know, what may be the cauſe thereof, when there appears no difference in the Laughter and occaſion of it?*

A. From the Reproduction of the one, and the Applauſe given to the other, we may plainly gather, that, as the ſame Effect may proceed from Different Cauſes, ſo *Sarah's* Laughter proceeded from Diſtruſt, but *Abraham's* was the Conſequent of Joy. And therefore, when the Text ſays, he Laugh'd, the Chaldee Paraphraſt renders it, he Rejoyc'd.

Q. *Is there two, or will there be at the Reſurrection any Females in Heaven, ſince there ſeems to be no need of them there?*

A. Since Sexes are Corporeal Diſtinctions, it follows, that there can be now no diſtinction of Sex in Heaven, ſince the Souls only of the Saints (which are Immaterial Subſtances) are as yet in that Happy Place. And that our Riſing Bodies will not be diſtinguiſh'd into Sexes, we may ſafely gather from thoſe Expreſſions of our Lord's, *In the Reſurrection they neither give, nor are given in Marriage, but are as the Angels of God.*

Q. *An humble Suitor comes to beg your favourable Aſſiſtance in the diſcloſing to him the Genuine Senſe of* Gen. 6. 2. The Sons of God ſaw the Daughters of Men, that they were fair, and they took them Wives of all which they choſe.

A. The Sons of God, were, the *Children of Seth*, who were the Holy Seed: And the Sons of Men were the Poſterity of *Cain*, who were a Prophane Generation.

The Author of this Queſtion ſhall, if deſir'd, have a Private Anſwer to his other Queſtion.

G g   Q His

Fig. 37. Page size 12½ × 7½ in.

publish only one part, for the customer had to buy the other parts elsewhere; but there was no space for all parts, so the music had to be discarded altogether and only words appeared. The cruellest blow was the late discovery in the editorial office that it would cost far more to organize such a concert than could ever be recouped from subscriptions. Pretexts were hastily drummed up. Would readers of the *Apollo* really care to mix freely with each other, his Grace and the Duchess with every coffee-man and his wife? In any case, it was declared, no hall of size sufficient to accommodate all readers could be found. With relief the proprietors extricated themselves from what might have been a ruinous adventure in the days before advertising support could be obtained.

The names and contents of two essay-papers of Queen Anne's reign have become familiar from studies in Eng. Lit.: the *Tatler* and the *Spectator*. When Steele founded the *Tatler* in 1709 he had in mind a magazine: contributions of 'Gallantry, Pleasure and Entertainment', of poetry and learning and of domestic and foreign news. This ambitious project dwindled to one essay and a few miscellaneous paragraphs; though it is fair to say that the essays written by Steele and Addison combined gallantry, pleasure and entertainment in a single composition. The *Tatler* was a bi-weekly, Wednesdays and Saturdays, a single sheet price 1d, newspaper size and layout. Steele confessed that he hoped to attract women readers, and he did attract advertising for women: cosmetics, such as 'an incomparable beautifying cream' for sunburn, 2s 6d a gallipot and sold, oddly enough, at a toyshop.

The *Spectator*, the joint production of Steele and Addison, was begun as a daily in March 1711, and from the beginning contained only an essay and readers' letters, often written in response to the essay.[6] This strikingly illustrates the difference between society in the early eighteenth century and our own day: there is no longer a market for a daily paper containing only entertainment, and superbly written though the *Spectator* was, it could not have survived except in the witty, sociable and sophisticated coffeehouse society of its period. And that such a daily paper could be supported was of consequence to the printers of London.

These printers had, of course, little influence or interest in the editorial policies of the sheets they printed. In general, the conductors of periodicals, whether of news or entertainment, had no connexion with the printing trade: they made a contract with the printer in the same way as their bookseller-cum-publisher contemporaries. But because periodical printing was involved, the economic circumstances were beginning sharply to differ. Whereas the bookseller had freedom to sell at a price that not only paid the printer's bill but included his own profit, the periodical proprietor had to sell at a minimum price, because he had to obey the first rule, that periodicals must be cheap. Thus, the contents of the periodical were important to the London printing trade, if not to the individual printer, because the success of the proprietors offered security for the settlement of the printer's bill.

Among these revenues advertisements had become of high importance: the *British Apollo* received as much from the insertions in each issue as from the sale of 100 copies, and the printing bill for those 100 copies, in the days of the hand press, was no small item. The usual charge for an insertion was 2s 6d regardless of length, but in a sheet devoted entirely to advertisements, the *Generous Advertiser*, the method of charging by length was employed, 3d for fifty letters. This enabled the proprietors to give the sheet away, hence the name *Generous Advertiser*, and they claimed a circulation of 4,000, greater than that of any contemporary with the exception of the *London Gazette*, at that time selling about 6,000. This charge of 3d must have been calculated upon the costs of composing, correcting and printing the fifty letters.

To attract the customers to the advertisers, typographical devices were employed. Fists ☞ had been much used in certain periodicals since the revival of news publishing. The invention of the first daily newspaper appears to have encouraged another invention: the use of advertisers' blocks. It is dangerous to claim a 'first', but certainly no leading periodical employed this device in the seventeenth century.

On March 17, 1703, almost exactly on the first birthday of the *Daily Courant*, the first advertisement block appeared in its columns. The drawing was simple, and the object more like a lanthorn than what it claimed to be: a chocolate-making-machine —the predecessor, perhaps, of the espresso. It is proper that the man who invented a machine should also have credit for another idea, a new method of selling; so proper that one has a sneaking hope he will not be displaced.

It was sensible to find a new method of presentation. Hitherto,

The Author of the New Invention for making Chocolate the finest and, cleanlieft in the World, Sells ALL NUT 3 s. a pound, Sugar and Nut. 2 s. a pound, to 3 pound a quarter of a pound Gratis. Six other Sorts at as reafonable Rates. 800 Inventions will be difpos'd of by Subfcriptions, to put by that laborious loathfom way of making up on a Stone, And that the Nobility and Gentry may be better fatisfied that there is none like what is made by this Invention, he makes at their Houfes 4 Days a Week, allowing him a Privacy, the working part being a Secret. The Invention is to be feen, and the Chocolate fold by none but the Author in Stropfon's Court in White-Fryers, the third Door behind the Green Dragon Tavern in Fleet-ftreet. Note, That none of his eight Sorts of Chocolate admits of Courfe or foul Settlings, as is ufual with others.

A Draught of the new Invention, no way 13 Inches all bright caft Iron.

Fig. 38. Inwood's advertisement in the *Daily Courant* (column width, 18½ picas) during March 1705.

books and patent medicines had dominated what now ranks as 'display' advertising, though the 'display' then amounted only to leading. No one seems to have tried to sell a machine through the columns of a periodical. The other branch of advertising, now called 'classified', consisted of notices of property, articles lost and found and situations vacant. The inventor of this chocolate-making machine was, therefore, breaking new ground.

From a statement in the first advertisement for the machine it appears that the contraption had been preceded by a similar one that lacked the merit of being 'no way 13 inches'. This feature, anyway, is the one to which importance was attached in the description, though it is not obvious why the size should be so peculiar an advantage to the chocolate-maker. The inventor continued to attach importance to the measurement, and the information was transferred from the text of the advertisement to a position below the block. Later advertisers realized that an advertisement block should not need a caption.

Having gone to the expense of the block, the inventor, who later revealed his name, Robert Inwood, consistently used the illustration. His first campaign was three insertions in the *Daily Courant*, Wednesday and Friday in one week, Thursday in the following. Mondays, Wednesdays and Fridays became the days he favoured, and he had the modern reluctance to advertise on a Saturday.

Presumably his new method was successful, for he undertook short campaigns three or four times a year, each with a new theme in the text—or, as the modern advertising agent would call it, the 'copy'. He advertised his change of address when he moved to Fleet Street—and hurriedly warned his public that the machines still being sold at his former address were counterfeits. In another campaign he promoted a special batch of 800 machines obtainable by a form of hire-purchase. In another he became violently anti-Semitic: a pound of his chocolate was claimed to be worth a cartload of 'that foul stuff sold by hawking Jews'. To be anti-Semitic he had to prove that he was himself English, and so he abandoned his anonymity.

Inwood's contemporaries did not immediately follow his example. For some time his only real rival was William Mason, the writing-master, and their fields were as different as their approach. Mason used the sign outside his shop as the basis of his

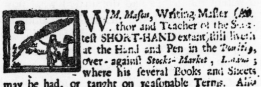

Fig. 39. William Mason's advertisement in the
Flying Post (column width, 17½ picas)
in the last months of 1704.

illustration. His first campaign opened in the *Flying Post* in January 1704, nine months after Inwood, and both remained faithful to their respective publications. Mason never had the idea of writing advertising 'copy', and so, although certain traits in Inwood may be disagreeable, his initiative in the use of block and 'copy' was remarkable.

There were spasmodic illustrated insertions by other advertisers: among the most strange to modern eyes was the surgeon, who tried to attract custom by a block that showed him in the act of operating on a waterman's wife. The block was too small to give more than a general impression of her complacency.

The next advance in advertising technique came in the second

the *Spectator* had sold three thousand, which was very good, and after the Stamp Acts daily newspapers could probably survive on smaller circulations if they attracted a liberal subsidy.

The most successful periodical founded after 1725 was the *Gentleman's Magazine* (1731). Here, at last, we have the word used in a title. Dr Johnson recalled that the *Gentleman's Magazine* had a circulation of ten thousand, which suggests that the extension of newspaper readership was of benefit to the literary papers though the *Gentleman's Magazine* was the first periodical to demonstrate that a large provincial circulation existed. But the proprietor, Edward Cave, was meticulous, as Johnson noted, in his care for readers: if he heard someone say that they would be ceasing to take the *Gentleman's Magazine*, he would instruct the editor to prepare a specially good number.

The contents were much on the lines of its predecessor, the *Gentleman's Journal*, and the successive literary papers: essays on a wide variety of subjects, articles and poems. The vast range of the *Gentleman's Magazine* is apparent from any list of contents: a monthly, price 6d, it was excellent value, and established a formula for a monthly periodical which lasted for a couple of centuries.

Cave, who was disguised under the pseudonym of Sylvanus Urban, Gent., used the word 'magazine' for a specific reason. A novel feature of his publication was the abridgement or précis of any important news item or essay that had appeared in the month's newspapers, London or provincial. Cave believed that 'a true specimen . . . [may be] as satisfactory as the whole parcel', and he supervised the writing of these summaries with the care he seems to have bestowed on all matters. The reports were thus 'treasured up' in a 'magazine' or store, and so Cave included in the title of his journal this word of significance, which was intended to differentiate his periodical from contemporaries. A list of the periodicals raided appeared on either side of the title-page block. The principle was a success; and still is so, as the *Reader's Digest* proves. Cave's purpose, however, had been to devise a formula that would not be liable to the stamp duty.

The *Gentleman's Magazine*, an octavo in blue wrappers, was reprinted many times in book form and it became usual for literary papers to perpetuate themselves in this format as books, and if necessary folios were reset as octavos and duodecimos.

Indeed, some literary papers existed as periodicals only until sufficient issues had appeared for a reprint in book size. These reprints had a great success: the *World* (Lord Chesterfield's *World*) in the mid-century ran for three years as a periodical and then went through ten London editions, two Irish and four Scottish. Nor was that the end: until 1829 it was appearing as part of a collection of essays, and in 1856 there was an American edition.[5] The *Tatler* and the *Spectator* were kept alive in the same way, and scarcely a year passed without an edition of one or the other.

The Charitable Mercury,

A N D

Female Intelligence.

Being A

Weekly Collection

O F

All the Material N E W S, Foreign and Domestick:

With some NOTES on the same.

To be Published Every Saturday.

Saturday, April 7. 1716.

Chi biasima i Grandi scorre pericolo ; chi li loda spesso dice la bugia.

IT is well enough known to the Publick, that I intended lately to entertain 'em with a Paper under another Title ; and I need not tell by what means I am prevented from pursuing my Design. However, the same Reasons still prevailing with me to accept of that Encouragement the Publick then intended me, and some worthy Gentlemen generously offering their Assistance in carrying on a Weekly Paper for my Benefit, emboldens me to attempt this Publication, and I hope for better Success with this than I had with my other Undertaking. These Gentlemen bid

Fig. 42. The masthead of the first, short-lived newspaper for women readers. Depth to the rule below the date, 4⅜ in.

Periodicals specifically intended for women were rare until the end of the century, though there was early an attempt to establish a newspaper. This was undertaken in 1716 by Mrs Elizabeth Powell. She acquired two fine blocks, one of a mother and children and one of a young woman, presumably unmarried, firmly grasping the anchor of hope, and these were placed in the masthead. Unfortunately, what was specially designed for women readers ceased with the masthead: Mrs Powell lifted all her news, without the slightest sub-editing, from the newspapers intended for men. Her venture survived only for the one issue.

In the mid-century there was the *Female Spectator*, a monthly periodical of chatty advice on etiquette, love and marriage and parent-child relationships. There were no separate articles, but to diversify the account the conductor (a woman) inserted stories, supposedly true, in which the heroines were disguised with exotic names such as Barsina and Amasina, Melissa and Alithea. Much of the advice was sound: girls should not be isolated from society, or they would become an easier prey to the wiles of men—'many a squire's daughter,' she pointed out, 'has clambered over hedge and stile to give a rampant jump into the arms of a young jolly haymaker or ploughman!'[5]

The periodical that was securely founded upon the love and marriage theme was the only one, then and now, that was likely to attract a wide feminine readership. The point was squarely put by the young lady who wrote to the editor of the *Mirror*, a late-eighteenth-century essay-paper: she was 'tolerably well pleased with his efforts', but she could 'wish it were not quite so grave, and had a little more love in it'.[9]

Publications by women for a general readership were more successful, and the most successful of all was the first Sunday newspaper, begun in 1779 by Mrs Elizabeth Johnson. Her *British Gazette and Sunday Monitor* consisted like Mrs Powell's *Charitable Mercury* of news lifted from the dailies, dignified only by the addition of a sermon. Yet it was welcomed by those who were reluctant or unable to buy the high-priced dailies, or who preferred to leave their reading—or their listening—to the week-end.

Mrs Johnson was a woman of considerable business acumen. The original idea was sound, and she understood that she must continually remind her readers that hers was the original Sunday newspaper. She also understood that circulation directly affected advertising revenue. In 1791, when she informed her public that she sold 4,000 copies a week, she noted it as a circumstance which 'must give a most pleasing sensation to all advertising customers'. In spite of her formidable typography, she had evidently hit on a successful device, and the idea of a periodical on the seventh day was quickly adopted.

Among men the notion persisted that women wished to be educated, would take lessons in history and geography and current affairs. Mr Jasper Goodwill of Oxford was so inspired when he began his *Ladies' Magazine* in 1749. It appeared from London, from Eliot's Court, opposite the Old Bailey, where Miles Flesher and John Haviland had once had a printing house.

The *Ladies' Magazine* was a fortnightly, Saturdays, 16 quarto pages for 2d. The page size allowed the matter to be set in two columns and in a reasonable type size—only on the title-page was small type set to the full measure, an effusion of Goodwill which, perhaps, the printer decided no one would wish to read. There was a concession to feminine taste in a row of fleurons below the masthead, a fashion imported from France where they had been revived by Pierre-Simon Fournier.

It is fair to suspect that the printer thought of the fleurons: Goodwill seems to have had little conception of what might appeal to women. For months the chief article was a history of England with much about the finances of the Plantagenet Kings—a hideous serial. There were other instructive articles on geography and botany and—the end crowns all—commodity prices, stocks and shares and a list of bankrupts. Match-making mammas may, however, have found the last item instructive. Goodwill had the audacity to subtitle his outrageous demand upon feminine tolerance: the *Universal Entertainer*.

It is true that in the eighteenth century the opportunities for a woman to acquire an education were restricted, but it passes belief that there was any real demand for Jasper Goodwill's pedantry, even when presented with flowers. After his short-lived venture the formula underwent sensible modification in a later publication, the *Lady's Magazine*, the first of several with this title. Here again were the printer's flowers, but now arranged by an expert hand. The paper was superior, and in the format (octavo) and typography there was a perceptible effort to produce a page that would please and attract.

The contents still included the succinct history of the present war in Germany, but at least it was 'succinct', and botany was transformed into flower culture. The opening article was a short story, such as 'The Sibil, a tale after the manner of the East'—at a period when anything Persian, Indian or Turkish was chic. Riddles and poems, a song with words and music, completed the variety. Lastly, there was an important inset: an engraved plate of, for instance, a woman in Elizabethan dress. The craftsmanship was excellent, but the subject is a shade didactic: one may be

mildly interested in the fashions of Tudor times, but they are not
so lively a talking-point as the fashions of the day. Nevertheless,
the idea of an engraved inset was to prove fruitful and the *Lady's
Magazine* was the first step towards the successful women's
magazine.

Engraving had been used for book title-pages since the beginning of the seventeenth century and for job printing since the
beginning of the eighteenth. By the 1740s it was being applied to
periodicals. Colour came later. One of the most elaborate
periodicals to have engraved insets was the *Botanical Magazine* of
1787, a portfolio of superb engraved, coloured plates. On the one
hand there was this example, a London publication, and on the
other, from France, came the application of the engraved and
coloured illustration to fashion. The *Cabinet des Modes* was
founded in Paris in 1785 and could be bought in London. And so
in 1790 there appeared the *Lady's Monthly Museum or Polite
Repository of Amusement and Instruction*. A fearsome title; but
in every other respect a periodical of delicacy and perception.
Significantly, it was conducted by a Society of Ladies. Here, at
last, was a magazine designed for the sprightly heroines of Jane
Austen. Undoubtedly, the section first explored was the
'Cabinet of Fashion'—a direct borrowing from the French
contemporary.

Every month two styles were shown, a walking dress and a full
dress, with a short description of each, including the accessories,
for the items would be made from the pattern by the reader's
own craftsmen. The illustration (see Plate XI*a*) shows a walking
dress 'of clear muslin, a deep lace let in round the bottom. A robe
of crimson satin edged round with white swansdown, full sleeves,
looped up with a diamond button. White muff, gloves and shoes.'
There was a similar short account of the full dress, but in this case
the hair also required attention: 'head fashionably dressed,
ornament with a silver wreath and heron's feathers'. The heron-
ries of the British Isles must have been decimated after this issue
reached the drawing-room.

Though not elaborate the colouring was careful and brilliant. It
was unfortunate that the page size of the *Monthly Museum*, a
duodecimo, was rather too small for these fashion plates to appear
in their full glory. There was also a rigidity about the models that
may derive from the botanical drawings that had preceded the

K

fashion plates; both, no doubt, being drawn by the same artists.

Other contents were vivacious. There were both short stories and serials of romantic interest with heroes either titled—Count was the rank preferred—or gallant soldiers of foreign birth, such as Don Pedro. 'Matchless woman!' Don Pedro exclaims to the heroine before he does battle against the Infidel, 'we shall succeed: thy virtues will crown us with victory.' On another occasion his lips 'tremulously' murmured 'Isabella!' Edifying and inspiring, perhaps, if hardly as instructive as Jasper Goodwill would have liked.

The *Monthly Museum* contained book reviews under the stern heading of the 'Literary Tribunal', and there was a section of poetry, the 'Apollian Wreath'. And there were playlets with characters such as 'Caroline Henderson, attached to Edward', that were undoubtedly acted in country houses like Mansfield Park. Finally, if the British Fair really thirsted for instruction, they could read a short biography of an eminent woman. There was correspondence, but the editress made no attempt to answer questions relating to 'love etc.' in the manner of the *Ladies Mercury* a century before. This was, perhaps, the only defect when the *Monthly Museum* is considered as the forerunner of the women's magazines today.

We have, unfortunately, no idea of the circulation of the *Monthly Museum*, but an earlier *Lady's Magazine* claimed one of 'several thousands'.[10] The monthly production of the colour plates must have been an anxiety. Before each sheet went through the press the engraved copper plate was coloured by hand, a process infinitely more laborious even than the hand press; and that was laborious enough. The incitement to mechanical invention was high. So long as the production of printed sheets depended on human muscle, not only for inking and feeding, but for moving the bed of type to and fro beneath the platen (or rolling back and forth), there could be little startling increase on a circulation such as Mrs Elizabeth Johnson had claimed for her *British Gazette and Sunday Monitor*—4,000. The hand press had scarcely changed since the days of Gutenberg. Nor had the format of books changed greatly. But there had been astonishing changes in periodicals and by the end of the eighteenth century this branch of the London trade was lively, thriving and inventive. Its greatest achievements were yet to come.

NOTES

1 The typographical changes in eighteenth-century newspapers are described and illustrated in *The English Newspaper 1622-1932* by Stanley Morison (Cambridge, 1932).

2 Graham Pollard, 'Notes on the Size of the Sheet', *The Library* (1941), xxii, 105.

3 Stanley Morison, *Ichabod Dawks and his 'News-Letter'* (Cambridge, 1931).

4 J. G. Muddiman, *The King's Journalist 1659-89*, an account of Henry Muddiman (London, 1923). Peter Fraser in *The intelligence of the Secretaries of State and their monopoly of licensed newsbooks, 1660-88* (Cambridge University Press, 1956) discussed the use made of the intelligence at the time. Maurice Ashley in *Cromwell's Generals* (London, 1954) and C. V. Wedgwood in *The King's War* (London, 1959) are modern historians who appreciate the value of newsbooks and papers.

5 Richmond P. Bond (editor), *Studies in the early English Periodicals* (Chapel Hill, 1958). The introduction by the editor gives an excellent account of magazines. One contribution is devoted to the *British Apollo*, another to *The Female Spectator* and a third to the *World* (Chesterfield's).

6 In *New Letters to the Tatler and Spectator* (University of Texas Press, 1959) Professor Richmond P. Bond has edited ninety-six letters, unpublished but preserved by the conductors of these journals.

7 F. S. Siebert, *Freedom of the Press in England 1476-1776* (Urbana, 1952).

8 A. Aspinall, *Politics and the Press c. 1780-1850* (London, 1949).

9 *The Mirror* (Burney 99), a bi-weekly essay-paper published in Scotland.

10 Graham Pollard, 'The Early Poems of George Crabbe and *The Lady's Magazine*', Bodleian Library Record (1955), v, 149.

VI

The Periodical Press from the Eighteenth Century to Modern Times

READERS are tolerant of bad printing in newspapers: whereas few book readers would welcome sheets on which the ink has not been allowed to dry, the occasional smudged issue of a newspaper can pass with the excuse that it is 'hot from the press'. In the past, heavy demands were made on this tolerance. In three centuries of news publishing and two of periodicals the English reader had seldom seen a decently printed sheet. John Wolfe provided some of the few exceptions, but not until the end of the eighteenth century, when the periodical press was on the verge of mechanical revolution, was there a keen interest in the printing and design of periodicals. The man responsible was John Bell.

This bright-eyed, red-faced, rather horsy looking man was indisputably the most versatile member of the London printing trade at any period. He engaged in all three branches—books, newspapers and jobbing—in itself a feat. He was his own typographer and designer. He established a type foundry. In addition, he edited, he acted as a foreign correspondent, and he wrote advertising copy. He set up a bindery, and he not only sold books but published them. He even planned to print the Book of Common Prayer—perhaps the most convincing illustration of his enterprise and self-confidence. No man has equalled his record.[1]

By the time he was 27 Bell was a newspaper proprietor, one of the syndicate of eleven who founded the *Morning Post* in 1772. He was already a bookseller and the trade resented his participation in newspapers: he was denounced as a piratical intruder, which suggests that by the last quarter of the century a gulf was

widening between the periodical proprietors and the book trade
—although it is true that Bell was never regarded with favour by
his fellow booksellers.

After fourteen years with the *Post* Bell sold his interest and
founded his own journal in partnership with an elegant man-
about-town, Edward Topham. Both agreed that the new journal,
the *World*, should contain 'fine writing and pleasantry'. To give
one example: in those days Parliamentary reporting was taken
seriously, as was proper when the right to report, so long contested,
was so recently won—but not in the *World*. The reporting there
was sprightly, even flippant: an Address at the opening of a
session was dismissed with, 'as usual, little more than an echo [of
the Speech] with the mere alternation of tense and person
transposed, and an animated readiness towards the requisite
supplies'. And there was in the *World*, as in the *Sunday Express*
today, a quick-witted interest in personalities rather than in
policies.

The *World* took advertising seriously, as its sub-title of
Fashionable Advertiser indicated. Bell, who was responsible for
the typography, devoted thought to the front page. He singled out
the subjects that would most appeal to the fashionable: opera, the
playhouse, fine arts, polite literature, and emphasized the
headings with a short rule, effectively placed so that it did not
detract from the legibility of the line above.

Bell's elegant typography has never been surpassed in a newspaper. Paragraphs were leaded so that the reader's eye was no
longer repelled by close print. He abandoned the long 'ſ'—it was
twenty years before the rest of the trade saw his wisdom—and he
embellished the columns with the discreet use of italics and
capitals. Admittedly, space was not at a premium in the *World*,
which did not attempt to be an inclusive register of events.

He was also responsible for the mock Gothic masthead, mock
because it had the white line and the further licence that attended
cutting as a block. There had been examples of blackletter in
mastheads because it was the blackest letter held by the printer:
he had, as yet no fat face, sans serif or slab serif. But the fashion
for mock Gothic dates from Bell.

When in 1932 *The Times* abandoned its blackletter masthead
there was a passionate outcry at the break with tradition—which
was nothing of the sort. Blackletter was not used in the masthead

of the *Daily Universal Register* (1785) or in January 1788 when this sheet was retitled *The Times*. It was copied later from the *World* as every other ambitious newspaper copied mock Gothic from the *World*. When Bell found he was being imitated he abandoned the face and introduced the outline roman capitals cut by Fry, an equally distinctive but more elegant design, one of the last contributions to display typography before the advent of the fat faces.

In 1789 Bell and Topham quarrelled, and the former founded his own competing daily, the *Oracle: or Bell's New World*. His typographical innovations appeared in this and also in his successful Sunday newspaper, *Bell's Weekly Messenger* (1796). Later, these periodicals, the daily and the Sunday, together with a monthly magazine, were running at the same time, in addition to Bell's interest in the book trade, although this had declined by the end of the century. But to be the active proprietor of so many periodicals was without precedent; and they were all successful, all making a contribution of some novelty.

He even found time to go abroad as the foreign correspondent of the *Oracle* in the wars that were eventually to throw a little Corsican into the first position in France. Bell actually marched with the French armies, and in his ambition to send home 'the earliest and most faithful intelligence', he made what he described as 'a perilous excursion' through West Flanders in order to be present at a battle. For his pains he was reviled by *The Times*, so he said later, as 'a bloody satellite of Robespierre'. This hurt him deeply. As in much else, he had set that newspaper an example of 'disinterested and uninfluenced integrity', and before his death it is to be hoped he realized how such integrity had become—and has remained—that newspaper's proudest boast.

In 1806 Bell began his remarkable women's monthly magazine, punningly entitled *La Belle Assemblée*. It owed much to French models and much to its predecessor, the *Ladies' Monthly Museum*, and much to Bell's own association, through Topham, with the fashionable world. But it was clear from the title-page that Bell was going to contribute something to the formula already devised for the *Monthly Museum*. The frame included supporters on either side, Egyptian-style figures with fanned-out headdress, carrying a final slab. Most chic: for fashionable interest in Egyptian antiquities would be reflected typographically within the next decade by the slab-serif design with its heavy finials. The *Monthly Museum* had preferred classical architecture and cupids on the title-page.

The *Monthly Museum* was elegant in the well-bred style of the English country-house party; the elegance in Bell's journal had a touch of the raffish, of international society. Significantly, he included paragraphs of current news with reports of fatal duels, and essays on the theatre in which, for example, Congreve's 'Mourning Bride' was rated above 'The Way of the World'. Original contributions were admitted if the style were chaste and elegant, and Bell, always a businessman, promised that when 'pecuniary recompense' was required, it would be 'liberally gauged'. No such inducement was mentioned by the conductors of the *Monthly Museum*.

The page size was larger than in the *Monthly Museum* and so Bell's fashion plates appeared to greater advantage. From the beginning his models were not static but in action, and more and more background detail was added. And altogether, there was more fashion than in contemporaries. The *Monthly Museum* had shown only the full dress and the walking dress; Bell's readers could examine any garment from morning wrappers to bathing robes, and the plates were more fully described.

The illustration (see Plate XI*b*) shows a morning walking-dress worn with a 'mountain hat of straw or Imperial chip, trimmed with jonquille ribbon', and gold hoop earrings. The Parisian full dress was of 'India muslin worn over a satin slip that had a rich border of ruby foil and gold embroidery', and the hair was dressed 'in Eastern style, formed of the cable braid, bound and twisted on the forehead in alternate bands and knots'. It was confined at the back with a caul of gold net. The Cossack spencer and cap were of 'lilac twill sarsnet, ornamented with silk frogs, cords and tassels of the same colour'.

The contribution made by John Bell to the development of the periodical press was great and significant; but, versatile as it was, valuable as it was, his contribution was surpassed by John Walter II, son of John Walter I, the founder of *The Times*.

This sheet had begun publication in 1785 as the *Daily Universal Register*, with nothing to distinguish it from contemporaries. Its total size was no larger than that of a single page of *The Times* today. The title was changed on January 1, 1788, but the policy of inclusive reporting was continued, and within thirty years this daily universal register was soundly established and ready to embark under John Walter II on an astonishing career.

By the time he became Chief Proprietor in 1810 the wooden hand press had been superseded in many newspaper offices by the iron Stanhope, a press that was stronger, more compact and slightly more speedy. The wooden press had produced only 250 sheets an hour printed on both sides of the paper, and since the large sheets being used for newspapers were twice the size of the platen, which bears the paper down on the inked type, two pulls were necessary to take one side through the press. John Walter saw that the steam power which drove the spinning jenny and other machines of the Industrial Revolution must be applied to the press.

The inventor of the steam printing press was Friedrich Koenig and the technician a fellow German, Andreas Bauer. Using a massive arrangement of gears, Koenig made it possible for the type bed to travel to and fro upon a belt. Two steam presses on this principle were built for John Walter and secretly installed in the Office of *The Times* towards the end of November 1814.

The application of power to the movement of the bed was not Koenig's only invention. Hitherto, the type had been inked by hand, using leather balls which needed frequent cleaning and renewal. In the steam press the ink was held in a central reservoir, and after preparation between a system of rollers it was passed over the surface of the type metal by a final roller. The whole laborious process of hand-inking could be discarded, and inking rollers have been an essential feature on power presses since Koenig's time.

Further, the sheets of paper were no longer pressed down on the inked type by the rectangular platen, the size of which had always restricted the size of sheet. Instead, they were carried over the bed on a cylinder, known as the impression cylinder, another feature of modern power presses. This cylinder at once made possible an increase in page size. Whereas in 1793 the type area of a page of *The Times* measured 69 by 93 picas, limited by the platen of the hand press, in 1819 it was 89 by 122 picas, and in 1825, 97 by 123.[2]

Then, lastly, there was the revolutionary speed, which had been Walter's main object: 1,100 sheets printed on one side every hour.

The wood block would not have survived the long runs of these Sunday newspapers, but the old practice of wood-cutting was little used after Thomas Bewick's successful revival of wood-engraving, in which the durable end-grain is handled with a graver to produce a white line. Books illustrated with Bewick's white-line engravings had begun to appear by the end of the eighteenth century, and once craftsmen had been trained the technique offered the periodical publishers a means of illustrating their products.

Wood engravings, still rare in daily newspapers, were immensely popular in magazines. In an attempt to encourage the working-classes to improve their condition, Lord Brougham founded in 1826 the Society for the Diffusion of Useful Knowledge, and since he was a man accustomed to use the periodical press to further his causes, it was not long before the Society launched into print; with the *Penny Magazine*.

Readers had much better value for their penny than they had ever had from the *Athenian Mercury* or the *British Apollo*. The many informative articles on such weighty subjects as the Elgin Marbles or the periodical press itself were enjoyed because they were liberally illustrated with engravings of high quality. Though the *Penny Magazine* contained none of the sensational elements of the Sunday papers, it satisfied the real thirst of the working-classes for 'instruction' agreeably presented. The circulation of the *Penny Magazine* was soon 200,000. This was the first six-figure circulation in the history of London printing, and more: that six-figure circulation doubled. It was twenty times the circulation of the *Gentleman's Magazine* a century earlier; and it could not have been achieved without the invention of Koenig and Bauer that had been sponsored by John Walter II.

☆

No ambitious periodical printer could be without a steam press, but it was *The Times* that took the initiative in building presses of ever greater capacity. Koenig and Bauer had returned to their own country soon after their success, and two British engineers, Augustus Applegath and Edward Cowper, were installed in Printing House Square, the Office of *The Times*. The problem of multiplying the number of sheets printed an hour was solved by the Applegath and Cowper four-feeder of 1828. Its appearance was

Fig. 45. The Applegath-Cowper four-feeder of 1828. (*a*) Bed of type; (*b*) impression cylinders; (*c*) inking rollers; (*d*) feeding; (*e*) distribution.

more revolutionary than its principles. It was a flat-bed machine, the type being carried to and fro beneath four impression cylinders. These were fed by four operatives on two levels. The numerous rollers and tapes in the central tower guided the sheets to the bed, and back, along further tapes, to the delivery points. In the illustration, the bed looks insignificant: it weighed three-quarters of a ton.

The limiting factor was that the press still had to be hand-fed. By using two levels Applegath and Cowper had ingeniously increased the number of persons who had access to the machine. The rate was 4,000 sheets an hour, a figure later somewhat improved and one thought miraculous. 'Such ease, rapidity and accuracy united,' rhapsodized the leading article that introduced the press, 'could hardly ever before be ascribed to any fabric constructed by the hand of man; neither is it now possible, we conceive, for the printing machine to receive any further improvement, or to arrive at a more complete degree of perfection.' Justifiably, Printing House Square was impressed—even open-mouthed—at the magnitude of its achievement. Less than twenty years earlier, the hand press, producing some 250 perfected sheets an hour had been the only possible method of multiplication of copies. It was within the lifetime of most persons at Printing House Square that the miracle of 2,000 sheets (4,000 unperfected) an hour had been accomplished.

The London printing trade was equipped to expand in a manner undreamt of at the end of the eighteenth century. The steam press made possible such titles as the *Family Magazine*, founded in 1834, actually short-lived, but illustrative of the new principle of finding a basis for mass circulation.[4] And whereas journals for gentlemen and for ladies had been long established, now the attempt was made to give children their own reading-matter.

William Cobbett had realized that there was a market among children, but had not himself exploited it. The first production for juveniles, the *Boys' and Girls' Penny Magazine* appeared in 1832. With eight pages for the penny, it contained entertainment in the form of two stories, one usually a fairy story, and instruction in paragraphs on, for example, natural history. These would be illustrated with simple drawings of animals—a lavish use of blocks unthinkable in the eighteenth century. The application of colour on the first page as a means of attracting the children was shrewd. These colours were not printed but added by hand, girls being employed at about 5s a week to slap on the three or four colours.

A last section of the periodical press, the trade and technical journals, began to flourish. Again, production was made possible by the steam press, itself a product of the same Industrial Revolution that was rousing interest in trade and technical subjects. Agriculture had one or two journals devoted to its interest at the end of the eighteenth century; now in the 1830s mining and engineering journals became numerous, besides a number of specialized journals relating to the railway boom (see Plate XII*a*).

The inclusion of plates in these publications became as essential as cards in packets of cigarettes before the second world war. Copper was being ousted by steel as the preferred surface for engraving, and lithography was popular in this country by the thirties.[6]

Whatever the title, plates were appropriate. The *Farmers' Journal* (1832) promised that monthly parts should be embellished with a handsome lithograph of the most eminent patrons of agriculture, though the proprietors cautiously qualified the promise by 'from time to time'. There were line engravings in the *Farmers' Journal*, though not often. When the first illustration, of a machine for cleaning corn, appeared some two months after the journal had been founded, the editor obliquely warned readers that no precedent was set: 'We have been at considerable cost in procuring a correct engraving . . . in order that the reader may more readily comprehend its operation.'

The *Railway Magazine* (1835) contained very fine engraved plates, not only reproductions of architectural features, bridges and so forth, but of inventions, such as the pneumatic rail, by which the 'train' was to be sucked along (see Plate XII*a*). There were also detailed maps.

The *Illustrated London News* (1842) was the most outstanding of all the illustrated papers and separate plates of subjects in aquatint and so forth were given away regularly. It was the first periodical to use the word 'illustrated' in the title, though in the early numbers the engravings were sparsely scattered through the pages. The example was, however, quickly imitated, and as soon as it had the stimulus of a number of 'illustrated' competitors the *Illustrated London News* became better value.

During the 1830s the hobbies periodicals were also undertaken. Whereas the *Botanical Cabinet* of 1815 had contained observations that were semi-scientific rather than practical, the *Floricultural Cabinet* of 1833 was intended for people who gardened. Its conductor—he was too modest to call himself an editor—was a nobleman's gardener, and he invited contributions from those who successfully grew plants, flowers being preferred and vegetables virtually ignored. He ran a correspondence column and reviewed other relevant publications, their plates being listed. Naturally, his own included a leaf of coloured flower drawings. Reviews, it should be added, were uncritical, and politely approving: the *Botanical Cabinet*, for instance, still in existence, was 'very neat', and its observations, 'of a religious character, are very appropriate, and calculated to lead the mind of man from nature to nature's God'.

This vein of morality was by no means confined to the conductor of the *Floricultural Cabinet*. It ran through most editorial effusions of the periodical press and was highly valued by readers. As early as 1824 it had been thought that 'the Periodical Press of Great Britain' was 'the most powerful moral machine in the world', doubt amid cries of acclamation, during the Great Exhibition of 1851.

That *The Times* should need an eight-feeder at all was a matter of chagrin to other newspaper offices. The half-hearted reduction in price after the lowering of the duty in 1836 had not achieved its object: a more equitable distribution of readers between the organs of the London newspaper press. Clearly, if the power of *The Times* were to be broken, the duty must be altogether abolished. This step was taken in 1855. It did injure *The Times*, because the removal of the duty meant the end of the privilege of free postage which the stamp had carried. Owing to the inventions of Applegath and Cowper, *The Times* regularly consisted of sixteen or more pages, whereas rivals contained only eight. *The Times* would be forced either to reduce its bulk or to increase the cost to subscribers.

John Walter III, the then proprietor, faced a terrible dilemma. To reduce the bulk would mean the sacrifice of the incomparable news service and of valuable advertising. It would make nugatory the invention of the new machines to speed printing. *The Times* refused to abandon the policy of inclusive reporting, and in the event the circulation did not suffer to the extent enemies had hoped.

The chief result of the abolition of the taxes on knowledge—the other taxes were repealed soon after—was no benefit to the London dailies. The provincial press, hitherto weekly, was able to turn to daily publishing, and many new organs were founded in a burst of prosperity that lasted for the rest of the century.

So little was the power of *The Times* and its circulation injured that after 1855 Printing House Square was busy with a new process and new machines to give even greater printing speeds. The process was stereotyping, by which an exact plate is made from a mould of the type in its forme. The advantage of stereotyping in newspaper production was the same as in Bible printing: it circumvented the laborious process of duplicate setting. But the plaster-of-mould used by Eyre and Spottiswoode at this period (see p. 94) was no use in Printing House Square: it was slow, expensive, and provided only one plate. A more durable material was needed, and John Walter III took into the office an Italian, James Dellagana, who in 1857 successfully made printing plates from a *papier mâché* mould of a page of *The Times*.

These plates offered a solution of the difficulties of printing from the vertical cylinder of the eight-feeder. Unlike type in a forme, a stereotype plate can be bent, and once Dellagana had made curved steroes, a horizontal cylinder became possible. A new American machine, the Hoe ten-feeder, was introduced into Printing House Square, with a horizontal cylinder suspended so that the feeders could work around it. When these arrangements were completed in 1861 the Manager of *The Times* noted in his diary that 'a new era' in the history of newspapers had opened.

But the Hoe still printed single sheets on one side only, sheets laid on by hand at the rate of about 1,000 an hour. Walter began to think of printing from a continuous roll of paper. Then the only manual operation remaining, the hand-feeding, could be abandoned. And once a press was fitted with cylinders carrying curved stereotypes, the roll could be led through the printing cylinders in such a way that both sides could be printed on the one run, i.e. perfected. These ideas were incorporated in the Walter Press, designed and built in Printing House Square in 1866, the true rotary, reel-fed perfecting press, and the first in this country.

The hand-made paper that was then in use had to be damped as it entered the machine. It was then led between the top pair of an impression and a printing cylinder, when four pages on one side were printed, and then through the lower pair, when the other side

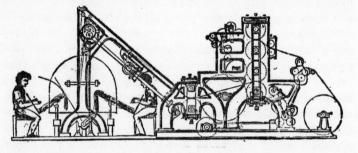

Fig. 48. The Walter Press of 1866. The small rollers projecting to the right damped the paper. Below them, slightly left, are the inking rollers for the lower pair of impression and printing cylinders (in the main tower). The second set of inking rollers are top left of the upper pair of cylinders.

of four pages was completed. Each printing cylinder had its own set of inking rollers. A cutter separated the continuous roll into sheets carrying eight pages. The sheets were taken up to the distributor, on which two takers-off were employed, alternate sheets falling to either side. Manned by only three men the Walter Press could produce 12,000 eight-page sections an hour. What an achievement this was! It was still less than a half-century since the hand press had been in use.

The principles of the Walter Press are fundamental to the present rotaries at Printing House Square and any other newspaper office. These only appear more complicated because of the web of paper and the folder, necessary to produce an entire copy of sixteen, twenty or more pages.

The introduction of rotary printing meant that at last composing must be speeded. Here, again, the initiative was taken by *The Times*. Other newspapers had not the circulations that demanded rotary printing, and in any case lethargy was forced on them by the trade unions. *The Times* was a non-union house throughout the nineteenth century: hence, it was able to adopt the Kastenbein composing machine. This was operated on a principle somewhat similar to the modern Linotype, in that the tapping of a keyboard released characters from a magazine. But actual type was released on the Kastenbein, not matrices as on the Linotype, and the sorts had to be justified by hand. So that fresh type could be used each day, the Kastenbein was worked in conjunction with the Wicks type-caster.

With these two inventions, rotary printing and mechanical composition, the periodical publishers could at last seek a mass circulation. A million readers could be supplied, and the *Daily Telegraph*, founded after the abolition of the taxes on knowledge, did dream of this figure. But if a million readers were to be found, they had to be sought among the classes that hitherto had not taken periodicals—for the excellent reason that they could not read; or could do no more than recognize letters and pick out individual words. And those who could read needed to be expert to cope with the formidable page of *The Times*, its close-set small type virtually unrelieved by headings. The *Daily Telegraph* and all the other London dailies looked equally formidable, and they failed to find a million readers.

The Education Act of 1870 removed an important disability

ANSWERS TO CORRESPONDENTS

☞ ON EVERY SUBJECT UNDER THE SUN. ☜

No. 1.   [Entered at Stationers' Hall.]   **JUNE 2ND, 1888.**   [European Postage, ½d.]   Price 1d.

"ANSWERS" IS PUBLISHED EVERY WEDNESDAY MORNING

The trade can obtain "Answers" from all wholesale agents and from the office,

26, Paternoster Square,

A LIVING CLOCK.

Dr. Willis mentions an idiot, who was accustomed to repeat the strokes of a clock near which he lived, with a loud voice. Afterwards having been removed into a parish where there was no church clock, he continued as before to call the hours successively; and this with so great accuracy, both as to the number of tolls, which he pretended to count, and as to the length of the intervening hours, that the family where he boarded conducted all their business by his proclamation of time.

ASS DRAWING WATER.

Some years ago an ass was employed at Carisbrooke Castle, in the Isle of Wight, in drawing water by a large wheel from a very deep well, supposed to have been sunk by the Romans. When his keeper wanted water, he would say to the ass, "Tom, my boy, I want water; get into the wheel, my good lad," which Thomas immediately performed with an alacrity and sagacity that would have done credit to a nobler animal; and no doubt he knew the precise number of times necessary for the wheel to revolve upon its axis to complete his labour, because every time he brought the bucket to the surface of the well, he constantly stopped and turned round his head to observe the moment when his master laid hold of the bucket to draw it towards him, because he had then a nice evolution to make, either to recede or advance a little.

SILK STOCKINGS.

Mezeray, the French historian, acquaints us that in 1559 Henry II. of France was the first who wore silk stockings in that country, at the marriage of his sister with the Duke of Savoy.

They are nevertheless said to have been worn in this country earlier, both by Henry VIII. and Edward VI. The latter was presented with a pair of long Spanish silk stockings by Sir Thomas Gresham.

Howell relates in his "History of the World" that Queen Elizabeth, in the third year of her reign, 1561, was presented with a pair of black knit silk stockings by her silk-woman, Mrs. Montague, and thenceforth she never wore cloth ones any more.

CONTENTS.

₀ Interesting answers are inserted in the paper; others go by post.

ORIGIN OF GROG.

The British sailors had always been accustomed to drink their allowance of brandy or rum clear, till Admiral Vernon ordered those under his command to mix it with water. The innovation gave great offence to the sailors, and, for a time, rendered the commander very unpopular among them. The Admiral, at that time, wore a grogram coat, for which reason they nicknamed him "Old Grog," etc., hence, by degrees, the mixed liquor he constrained them to, universally obtained among them the name of 'Grog.'

HAIR POWDER.

Hair powder was introduced by some ballad singers at the fair of St. Germains, in 1614. In the beginning of the reign of George I. only two ladies wore powder in their hair, and they were pointed at for their singularity. And at the coronation of George II. there were only two hairdressers in London. But in 1795, it was calculated that there were in the kingdom of Great Britain fifty thousand hairdressers; and supposing each of them to use one pound of flour in a day, this upon an average amounted to 18,250,000 pounds in a year, sufficient to make 5,314,280 quartern loaves.

ECCENTRIC CHARACTER.

The Rev. Mr. Hagamore, of Catshogs, Leicestershire, was a very singular character. He died the 1st of January, 1776, possessed of the following effects, viz.:—£700 per annum, and £1,000 in money, which (he dying intestate) fell to a ticket-porter in London. He kept one servant of each sex, whom he locked up every night. His last employment of an evening was to go round his premises, let loose his dogs, and fire his gun. He lost his life as follows: Going one morning to let out his servants, the dogs fawned upon him suddenly, and threw him into a pond, where he was found breast high. His servants heard his call for assistance, but being locked up could not lend him any. He had 30 gowns and cassocks, 100 pair of breeches, 100 pair of boots, 400 pair of shoes, 80 wigs (yet always wore his own hair), 58 dogs, 80 waggons and carts, 80 ploughs (and used none), 50 saddles, and furniture for the ménage, 30 wheelbarrows, so many walking-sticks that a toyman in Leicester Fields offered £8 for them, 60 horses and mares, 200 pickaxes, 200 spades and shovels, 74 ladders, and 249 razors.

Fig. 49. The typography closely followed that of *Titbits*.

as well as offering encouragement, and in 1881 the first periodical specifically designed for the barely literate came into existence: George Newnes' *Titbits from all the Most Interesting Books, Periodicals and Newspapers of the World*. Everything was short. The type was slightly larger than usual. Pages were broken up. The extracts were lively. *Titbits* could be read by people who were not used to concentrating on printed matter for more than a few minutes at a time.

The example of Newnes was followed by Alfred Harmsworth, later Lord Northcliffe, in an even more successful publication, *Answers to Correspondents on Every Subject Under the Sun*, a cumbersome title that, following Wolfe's example, Harmsworth shortened—to *Answers*. Brevity was basic, and like *Titbits*, *Answers* flitted from subject to subject—much the same technique as that of the *Athenian Mercury* and the *British Apollo*. People like snippets of information: that was why the question-and-answer paper had been so popular at the beginning of the eighteenth century. And it was even more popular at the end of the nineteenth, because Harmsworth leavened his instructive paragraphs with jokes. This formula of brevity in all things, instruction in some and humour in most has since been applied to the most successful publication in the world today: *Reader's Digest* with a global circulation of around 18 million.

Neither *Titbits* nor *Answers* was liberally illustrated and in appearance they had not much in common with the modern magazine. And No. 1 of the *Daily Mail*, which Harmsworth founded in 1896, was typographically in closer relationship to the eighteenth century than to the twentieth; although it was the first newspaper to reach the circulation of one million. Harmsworth was equipped to compose and print, but only after 1896 did the development of the half-tone process make it possible liberally to illustrate periodicals. The process of blockmaking was the last to receive the attention of the inventors.[7] After the beginning of the twentieth century the speed and cheapness of process-engraving transformed the periodical press, and when associated with big, black headline types, the nineteenth-century jobbing faces which had travelled to America and back to this country, gave us the modern newspaper.

The speed of process-engraving was only relative. The photographic negative must be printed down on a light-sensitive, coated plate and the image etched to a depth that will stand up to the pressures of stereotyping. Because the making of illustrations for periodicals of mass circulation has remained a major preoccupation of the London printing trade, two of the most recent inventions, the Klischograph electronic engraver, which circumvents the etching method, and the Lithotex (or Dirats) powderless etcher, developed for photo-composition, are contributions that will effect further changes. Both machines show a remarkable reduction in the time required for blockmaking.

It was, perhaps, the beginning of the end of the London newspaper printing trade when in October 1958 *The Times*, which had introduced both the Klischograph and the Dirats, began to print the Toronto *Globe and Mail* from Dirats plates made from pages of type set in Canada.[8] Art reproduction pulls are flown from Canada and the sixteen-page plates can be made on the Dirats in a few hours, a speed unthinkable in process-engraving. The centuries-old organization of a London printing house, with the composing and pressrooms under one roof, has begun to disintegrate.

By the end of the second world war many periodical houses had found it economically prudent to print in the suburbs. The national daily newspapers have been forced to remain in the capital; and must do so as long as last-minute news makes necessary alterations at the stage when the page is in chase, that is, the type is locked up preparatory to moulding; and as long as the railway terminals at King's Cross, Waterloo, Euston, Paddington and Liverpool Street are used for distribution. The day has not yet come when the last branch of the printing trade to be substantially represented in the capital can plan to depart, nor in our day will newspaper printing in London become a legend; whereas the London book printing houses are now forgotten sites and the job printers require the incentive of freeholds or of firm contracts.

NOTES

1 Stanley Morison, *John Bell 1745-1831* (Cambridge, 1930). A reproduction from *La Belle Assemblée* shows a lady in bathing robe.

2 *History of 'The Times'* (London, 1939), i, contains an account of the steam press. There are excellent collotype reproductions of pages of the newspaper in *Printing 'The Times' Since 1785* (London, 1953). Further illustrations and details of the various presses described in this chapter can be found in Lucien Neipp, *Les Machines à imprimer depuis Gutenberg* (Paris, 1951), and in John Southward, *Progress in Printing and the Graphic Arts during the Victorian Era* (London, 1897).

3 A. Aspinall, *Politics and the Press c. 1780-1850* (London, 1949).

4 *The Cambridge Bibliography of English Literature* (Cambridge, 1941), ii, 656, lists the vast number of periodicals that began to flourish at this period.

5 The periodicals mentioned in the following paragraphs can be seen in the British Museum and, in some cases, at St Bride's.

6 *The Periodical Press of Great Britain and Ireland: or an Inquiry into the State of Public Journals chiefly as regards their Moral and Political Influence* (London, 1824).

7 The several Printing Supplements published by *The Times* (1912, 1929 and 1955) contain useful accounts of the development of process blockmaking.

8 The production of No. 1 of the London weekly edition of the Toronto *Globe and Mail* is described in *Penrose Annual*, vol. 53, (London, 1959).

VII

Jobbing

THE last branch of the London trade to develop, 'job' printing has always been overshadowed by books and periodicals. Jobbing may be a useful sideline in a printing house, but rarely has a printer achieved either fame or fortune when he relied solely upon this miscellany of short runs.

It is more difficult to give a precise account of jobbing than of the other two branches, because the items are not invariably dated or traceable to a printer, and because relatively little jobbing has survived. Too often, cards or sheets or handbills may be used for one occasion or for a limited period, after which they are thrown away. Only two people in this country have made determined efforts to collect specimens of jobbing. The first was John Bagford, who was making his great collection, now in the British Museum, during the last decades of the seventeenth century and the first of the eighteenth. The other was John Johnson, Printer to the University of Oxford, who between 1925 and 1946 was active in forming a collection far greater than Bagford's which is now preserved at the University Press, Oxford.

There are small collections of individual items—playbills, ballads, matchbox labels and so forth, some of which can be seen by the public, others being in private hands. With these exceptions jobbing is unexplored territory and little has been written on the subject.

The collections of Bagford and Johnson are, therefore, of the utmost importance. Both men were beset by the mania for collecting, the true mania which will permit nothing to be thrown away. There are snags to an examination of Bagford's: he mutilated items to secure a decorated initial or a block, and stuck the pieces in his scrapbooks without dating or identification.

A venial sin was that he trimmed everything, so that margins have disappeared. But these are minor drawbacks to a fascinating achievement. He has been described as 'the most hungry and rapacious of all book and print collectors', who 'in his rage . . . spared neither the most delicate nor the most costly specimens'— indeed a bibliographical villain.[1] The truth is far from that. His collection offers a conspectus of typography that is more broadly based than Stanley Morison's *Four Centuries of Fine Printing* or D. B. Updike's *Printing Types*, because into his albums went everything good, bad and indifferent, whatever its condition; and so the marching pages record the styles, designs and types that were impressed on paper in Europe during two centuries.

The range of jobbing is so great that it would be possible to confine the following pages to a single subject, such as printed games. In attempting a more general account, examples must be selected here and there from each period. There is, however, a clear beginning, since Caxton printed the first known piece of London jobbing, an indulgence completed before December 13, 1476. Typographically, the single sheet that opens the history of the printing trade in London is not remarkable: it is the conventional legal form with its characteristic length of line and lack of paragraphing, but it represents a contract the execution of which would be economically attractive to a printer as yet unestablished. More interesting is the handbill or poster produced a year or so later (illustrated in D. B. Updike's *Printing Types*, vol I).[2]

Caxton made no effort to catch the eye with what we call 'display': the handbill is set in book type to book measure, and he adroitly took advantage of this, pointing out that the book of devotion which he was advertising was 'imprinted after the form of this present letter'. As 'advertising copy' the text of the bill is excellent: Caxton said precisely what he had for sale, described it, stated where it was to be had and concluded with a winning appeal to the pocket—the book is 'good cheap'. It is not known whether his method of publicizing his books was imitated: this seems to be an isolated example, as Richard Faques' *Trewe Encounter* is an isolated example of an early newsbook. Booksellers may have displayed loose title-pages in their shops, and Bagford may have collected many of his title-pages from this source for they were certainly stuck up in the eighteenth century, when

Pope refers to seeing his own name on a red and black title-page posted in a shop.

In the circumstances of sixteenth-century London printing it would have been difficult for jobbing to develop. The restriction on the number of presses was the crucial factor. Though the compositors complained of lack of work, the pressmen were always busy. The pressroom was the bottleneck; and would remain so. Christopher Barker I, the Queen's Printer, complained in 1582 of the difficulty in maintaining a smooth flow of Proclamations, which rank as jobbing, to his presses—and he had six. Bynneman may have done a little jobbing since he had the matrices for the secretary which was used on forms. When John Wolfe became Printer to the City in 1593 he virtually gave up news publishing, even though he had more than the permitted number of presses, in order to concentrate on the customs forms, passports, recognizances, notices of City Company meetings and so forth that certainly were produced by his successors. Wolfe may have initiated much of this jobbing, since before his time the City does not seem to have been aware of the amount of job printing it could sustain.

Lastly, for much of the century there were still alive many of the survivors of the old Stationers' Company, the professional writers who would have found employment in penning notices and forms. Not until the Civil War does there seem to have been a general demand for printed jobbing. But the lifting of restrictions on printing and the troubled circumstances after 1640 enabled jobbing to flourish. Nicholas Bourne, formerly Nathaniel Butter's partner in periodical publishing, sold jobbing: bills of lading, indentures, IOUs, licences and engravings and portraits.[3]

There was an urgency about the situation in 1640 and afterwards that was favourable to jobbing: old orders were being annulled overnight and new ones had quickly to be published. Printing was an important adjunct to Government by Parliament and Protector. There was an increase in the number of documents needed, and they had to be produced at speed; and when more presses were in operation than ever before it was possible to print such documents.

Early forms were set in book types, and book layouts were used, as they had been used at first for periodicals. There was no effort to lay the material out except as a piece of book composition.

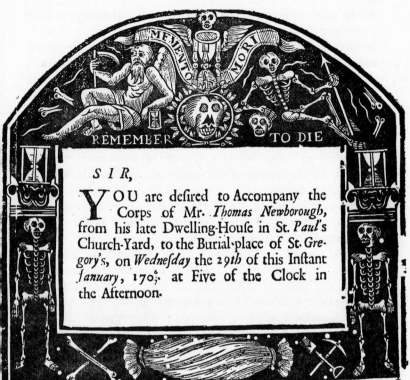

MEMENTO MORI

REMEMBER   TO DIE

S I R,

YOU are defired to Accompany the
Corps of Mr. *Thomas Newborough*,
from his late Dwelling-Houfe in St. *Paul's*
Church-Yard, to the Burial-place of St. *Gre-*
gory's, on *Wednefday* the 29th of this Inftant
January, 170⅚. at Five of the Clock in
the Afternoon.

Fig. 50. Width of block 6 in.

The idea of a form containing text divided up by rules into
columns which could be filled in under separate headings began
to develop only towards the end of the seventeenth century.

The final removal at that time of all restrictions on the trade
gave a considerable impetus to jobbing. Yet some of the first
eighteenth-century examples hark back to designs of the past. The
funeral card offers a striking instance. The execution is crude and
the style reminiscent of the gravestones and memorial tablets in
and about the churches of the early seventeenth century. Yet
these cards were produced in quantity at the beginning of the
eighteenth century and were popular among the middle-class.

As the eighteenth century advanced there was less obvious
relish in the minutiae of burial. The theme of the Resurrection
came into favour, and the cut of the souls rising at the Last Day

would often be accompanied by a simple representation of the procession. Hogarth engraved funeral cards of soberly dressed, bewigged gentlemen following the coffin. By Pitt's death, towards the century's end, the classical influence demanded a draped figure mourning over a tomb (see Plate XIII). The two winged skulls fluttering in the border are a last reminder of the activities of the worm and resurrection. In the nineteenth century, when it became usual for the undertakers to send out the cards, the preference was for mourning borders and a spray of lilies of the valley or other funerary flowers, a preference that still persists. In the course of the eighteenth century there was a switch from letterpress to engraving. The woodcut used on a funeral card has now a bizarre charm, but to polite society in its own day such a block may well have seemed as vulgar as some specimens from the nineteenth century to our eyes—for example, a funeral card of the 1860s, with a postage-stamp size reproduction in colour litho of the deceased, a fireman, resplendent in helmet and gold epaulettes. The clumsiness of the wood-block cutter and the inferiority of presswork on the hand press no longer satisfied a society accustomed to the engraved title-page. As the reigns of the first Georges passed, letterpress jobbing became a poor relation and it was engraved jobbing that was prepared for and handled by the fashionable world.

There were economic reasons for the increase in engraving. The printers wanted to keep their rolling press at work after the engraved title-pages had been worked off: they had therefore to create work. In this they were helped by the introduction in calligraphy of the round hand. Secretary was less and less used after the Restoration, just as blackletter, with which it had much in common, was abandoned for all work except royal proclamations and certain passages in legal or official documents or for restricted use in 'display'.

The round hand was admirably suited for engraving, and indeed it was through its development by the engravers that it became the 'copperplate' familiar to us. There were no further attempts to chip roman lower-case and roman capitals complete with serifs on the surface of a wood block. The flowing but simple lines and flourishes of the round hand triumphed, with capitals in small sizes delicately seriffed to give variation.

The engravers' skill was well demonstrated in the cards put

Susannah Fordham att the
Hartichooke on y Royall Exchange.
Selleth all Sorts of fine Poynts, Laces, and
Linnens, & all Sorts of Gloves, & Ribons,
and all others Sorts of Millenary Wares.

Fig. 51. An engraved tradesman's 'card' $7\frac{1}{2} \times 4\frac{3}{4}$ in.

M

Fig. 52. 3⅛ × 3⅞ in.

out by tradesman for self advertisement, an example of jobbing that has survived in quantity. Though they are commonly known as trade cards, they were not printed on card but on paper and vary considerably in size. Often the design included an illustration of the sign outside the shop, for since London streets were not numbered until the mid-century this sign played the same part in reminding the customer of a certain tradesman that the trademark does today.

Hundreds of these cards, examples from every imaginable trade, have survived, though no one except Bagford was much interested in them until John Johnson and Sir Ambrose Heal began to collect them in the present century.[4] Engravers were, of course, qualified to produce the finest for themselves, although every trade secured more elaborate display as the century proceeded and the transition to copperplate calligraphy was completed.

The engraver's card here illustrated (see Plate XIII) is interesting for the vignettes of the rolling press and the hand press, from which we may deduce that Messrs Dicey had both in the printing house. We know that both presses were kept at Oxford after the

Sheldonian Theatre was equipped for printing in 1669. Then, the rolling press cost only £5 1s 6d, whereas the hand press and furniture cost just under £29. The running expenses of the rolling press would be high, however, both because the plates themselves were costly and the craftsmen were highly skilled.

These cards formed only a small part in the vast range of engraved jobbing. Banks used engraving for promissory notes, and each town had its own bank and its own designs. The command-of-hand scrolls on demand notes and certificates are the beginning of security printing in the protection they offered against the forger's skill. Receipts were engraved, share certificates were engraved, the immense volume of highly speculative traffic in the South Sea stocks that culminated in the bursting of the bubble was undertaken on forms of the utmost dignity and substance. The rolling press served the expansion of British commerce throughout the world as effectively as the hand press had sustained Parliament's demands for the observances of its rights and privileges in the preceding century.

Fig. 53. $2\frac{1}{4} \times 2\frac{1}{4}$ in.

The eighteenth century, the age of elegance, was the age of engraved jobbing. How sharply this is brought home when we compare the theatre tickets collected by Bagford with those we clutch today! Holding the ticket for the first gallery one could not fail to imagine that one's clothes were immaculate, one's hands well manicured and oneself sophisticated. This was the sort of theatre ticket that Dryden may have held and Pope certainly did and no doubt, at a later period, Sheridan. The eighteenth century was a period when engraved jobbing had nothing of which to be ashamed: it could stand comparison with the best of book and periodical printing of any period.

The story of letterpress jobbing was different. We have a foretaste in the advertisement of one of the first printers to concentrate on jobbing, Richard Newcomb. His 9 point may be a handsome character, but the alignment and spacing are careless, inking is poor and type is broken. It is a wretched piece of advertisement

Advertisement

RICHARD NEWCOMB, Printer, from Bla~~~~~~rs, now liveth in the *Great Old-Baily*, at the Sign of the *Dyers-Arms*, near the *Sessions-House* : ⁔ Where he Printeth all sorts of Books, Bills, Funeral-Tickets, Acquittances for the Kings Tax, with all other things, *considerably Cheaper* than any Printer in *London*.

And what I undertake, shall be Printed on a handsom Character, (and Correct,) not to be mended by any of the Trade.

Fig. 54. $1\frac{1}{2} \times 2\frac{3}{4}$ in.

for his composition and presswork when compared with the trade card of Messrs Dicey, engravers. Newcomb found work because engraving was costly for short runs: many of the back-street tradesmen were content for him to print off handbills that could be displayed in a shop or distributed in the street. Indeed, Newcomb's standards were relatively high—other job printers were far worse, and perhaps understandably so if they believed the sheets would be kicked into the gutter within a few hours. They had little more incentive than newspaper printers today who keep the fish-and-chip merchants supplied with wrapping paper.

From what survives it would appear that during the eighteenth century there was letterpress jobbing for the poor man and engraved for the rich. An example of the latter is the superb receipt used by Robert Dodsley, the leading bookseller to polite society, for subscriptions to a work he proposed to publish (see Plate XIV*a*). Nothing could be more agreeable than these pulls from the actual copper engraving to appear in the book, completed by the text of the receipt enclosed in an ornamental frame. A subscriber was given a delicate intimation of the pleasure to come.

Advertisements for books, which would be placed in the shop or its window, were printed letterpress in Bagford's time and after. There was little variety in the setting. Trimmed sizes were generally small, about 5 by $3\frac{1}{2}$ inches, and were almost invariably set either in double pica (24 point) when the measure was too narrow, or in long primer (10 point) when it was too wide. The failure to lead the lines made the long primer particularly un-

This Day is Publiſh'd,

ONE Hundred of the *TATLERS,* Written by *ISAAC BICKERSTAFF,* Eſq; Printed in a Neat Pocket Edition, on the ſame Paper, and with the ſame Letter as this Advertiſement. Printed and Sold by *H. Hills* in *Black-Fryers,* and *J. Baker* at the *Black Boy* in *Pater-Noſter-Row.* Price Bound in Calves Leather, Four Shillings.

N. B. A Set of the Half-Sheet Brown Paper *Tatlers,* that come out Weekly, with all their Faults, are Sold for above Double the Price, beſides Binding.

HUDIBRAS in a Neat *Pocket* Edition, finely Printed, and Illuſtrated with Nineteen Cutts, beſides the Author's Effigies,. taken from the Original. The Cutts are Deſign'd and Ingrav'd by the beſt Maſters. Price Bound in One Volume, 4 s. In Three Volumes, 5 s. and may be had at the above-mention'd Places.

Fig. 55. $2\frac{7}{8} \times 5\frac{1}{2}$ in.

attractive to the eye. Capitals alone were rarely used: upper and lower-case, usually in italic, were preferred for a heading or for emphasis. There was little to make the heading, the word 'advertisement', compel attention either typographically or by content. There were some examples with printers' flowers, either as a complete frame or set in a row top or bottom; but nothing to rival the floriations of the engravers.

Whereas Dodsley and his colleagues conceived jobbing that was purposefully designed in every respect, and with the co-operation of the engraver attractively executed, the letterpress printer had failed to adjust himself to the idea that jobbing was a separate branch of the trade. He did not realize—or if he did, he rejected the notion—that there was an opportunity to use new layouts, new type designs and ornamental material, to make a lively approach to the reader. He was unable, or unwilling, to break away from the traditions of book design.

Among the handbills collected by Bagford only those put out by Richard Steele to publicize the bound volumes of the *Tatler* appear to have been deliberately designed as handbills and also deliberately designed to be distinctive. A consistent typographical style was adopted with generous leading and the result reaches a standard that was rare in the jobbing of the early eighteenth century. The credit, in all probablity, must go to Steele rather than to Henry Hills jun., and it may be significant that the former's links with polite society were close.

The efforts of Steele proved that without re-equipment letter-

Fig. 56. Size of plate $6\frac{1}{16} \times 8\frac{5}{8}$ in.

press jobbing could reach standards comparable with engraved work, but in the early years of the century few were eager to follow Steele's initiative. Handbills continued to be set solid and virtually unparagraphed. The royal device was often set at the head, though it might have no conceivable connexion with the tradesman, but was perhaps the only block the printer had to hand. Coarsely cut blocks were becoming the prerogative of quack doctors and such fry who could, presumably, afford to provide them, and a number of gruesome blocks survive of tooth extractions and operations.

Red was sometimes used, not as a second colour but alone, and a poor, thin red it usually was, not the superb colour that burns with black on Continental title-pages. These eighteenth-century letterpress job printers had not begun to think in terms of two-colour printing, and it would be a long time before they did.

The restrictions, so recently lifted, that had for so long crushed and crippled the trade may have been partly responsible for the depressed state of letterpress jobbing. Books and period-icals kept most printing houses busy. The Royal Printing House in Blackfriars did, however, in one respect set an interesting example. The illustration (Fig. 56) shows the fine keepsake given to 'Dr' John Bagford after a visit just before his death. It is difficult to believe this was the first visit, since he was a local man, born in the parish, who had spent his working life as a cobbler in the immediate neighbourhood of the royal Printing House. On the contrary, he and John Williams (see p. 91) the manager, must have been intimately acquainted and it is not impossible that Bagford may have incited Williams to the production of small pieces of printed matter such as keepsakes. They were also given to visitors to the University Press, Oxford, and that design was imitated by the printers who moved their shops on to the ice when the Thames froze up and did a profitable trade with people who liked to see their names in print.

In general, however, both the Bagford and Johnson Collections reveal that during the eighteenth century the letterpress printers made little effort to extend the range of jobs, or to encourage a customer to spend money with the printer in the hope of recovering the cost with a profit.

One line was well established in the course of the century. Certain petty officials and tradesmen began to send to their 'worthy masters and mistresses' reminders that a Christmas box should be forthcoming. One London firm who specialized in this trade, Reynells, claimed they started their series for beadles and bellmen in 1735, and they were still printing the appeal of the beadles and the sub-inspectors of nuisances in 1879.

The appeal was a single sheet printed on one side, but by the 1790s the size was impressive: about 21 by 17 inches—the increased size of sheet being used by the newspapers had been taken up by the job printers. At the head was a block representing the beadle and bellmen passing officially through the parish with fames trumpeting their progress. The frame was completed with roughly cut blocks illustrating up to eighteen episodes from the life of Christ. Below the heading block was the name of the parish of the beadle making the appeal. The interior of the sheet was filled with verses, which were varied from year to year on a permutation system. These verses were rhetorical addresses to a great range of persons and subjects: saints—St Crispian earned a place—Christmas itself and each of the Twelve Days, the customers, the royal family, and certain national or international figures—Napoleon qualified in the year of Waterloo. Some reputable poets contributed: Leigh Hunt wrote verses on slavery while he was in prison.

THE
Newsman's Present *to his* worthy Customers,
ON THE
Entrance *of the* New Year, 1761.

AGAIN the year returns with smi-
    ling face,
    To cheer each heart, enliven ev'ry
      Place ;
    The seasons, hours, and elements
      pursue
Their wonted course, still wonderful and true ;
Rouzes each bard who boldly dare aspire,
To mount *Parnaffus* in poetick fire.
In prose or rhyme their annual tribute pay,
And greet its presence with a joyful lay.
Permit me then kind Sirs in welcome song,
Again to mingle with the tuneful throng ;
No hard strain'd words are found to cramp my theme,
I never drank, alas ! of learning's stream ;
O'er the huge volume never por'd my eyes,
Nature alone my feeble verse supplies.
No impious thoughts this virgin paper stain,
To stir up vice and folly's right maintain.
Though want and painful servitude my lot,
A virtuous mind and gratful heart I've got.
Your servant's labours do not then refuse,
Accept with joy, with candour too perufe.
Though winter comes in frozen fetters bound,
Whose hoary head with isicles around.
Though rattling hail and drenching rains descend,
And winds and hurricanes the welken rend ;
Though sultry *Phœbus* darts his scorching beams,
While fainting mortals seek the cooling streams ;
Though thunder rowls, and forked lightenings fly,
Yet does your slave these dangers still defy ;
Withstands the fury of the cold and heat,
To bring in time the entertaining sheet.

From me you learn how *Pruffia's* mighty King
Makes ev'ry nation with his triumphs ring ;
How vaunting *Daun* when *Frederick's* trumpets sound,
Flies like the frighted deer before the hound ;
How rugged *Ruffians* too with dastard fears,
Run like their bears, and shake their shaggy ears.

How haughty *Gallia* pines with grief and shame,
At *Britain's* glory and great *George's* name ;
How *Albion* smiles to see proud *Lewis* fret,
How *Maubert* crams with lyes his false *Gazette*.
How *Pitt's* wise councils through the will of fate,
From sure destruction sav'd our tott'ting state.
With grief, alas ! I told the fatal hour,
When our late *King* was forc'd to feel death's pow'r,
So brave a *Monarch*, merciful and just,
But Kings and subjects must return to dust.
Not all their armies when combin'd can save,
The much lamented *Sovereign* from the grave.
In sable clad, *Brittannia's* sons appear,
On ev'ry eye-lid hangs the briny tear,
With heaving sighs they cry " and ishe dead,
" Ye cruel fates why did you cut the thread ?
" May choirs of angels guard his silent tomb,
" Till the last trump proclaim the final doom.
" In Heav'n plac'd, may then look down and see
" His *Grandfon* aiming to be great as *He*."
Hear laureil'd bards, his manly virtues sing,
A tender parent in a youthful *King*.
To all the busy town my toil conveys
Elections, races, poetry and plays,
Deaths, weddings, flocks, addresses to the throne,
Bankrupts and books, with cures for gout and stone,
With other matters which from chit chat rise,
When tattling *Fame* on full tongu'd pinions flies.
    You who in novelty take most delight,
The LONDON SPY your notice does invite ;
Or if in history you pleasure find,
READ's WEEKLY JOURNAL will supply your mind.
But should you like of ev'ry dish to eat,
St. JAMES's EVENING POST's a glorious treat.
    And now my yearly carrol's at an end,
May bounteous heav'n all its bleffings send ;
Peace, health and virtue dwell within your breast,
And pity always be a welcome guest.
Then may I hope your charity will flow,
That I my gratitude with thanks may show.

BRITANNIA PRINTING-OFFICE, White-Friers, Fleet-Street.

Fig. 57. Size 13⅛ × 8⅛ in.

In 1830 the cost of these sheets to the beadle was 200 or more at 5s 6d a 100 or, for a hundred only, 6s. He could have hardly failed to show a profit on this investment. And so, no doubt, did the printer, repeating the blocks and many of the verses for over thirty years.

Outside London the lamplighters—the 'careful' lamplighters —of Norwich adopted this idea. In the late eighteenth century their appeals were elegantly set verses on the subject of their toil in the replenishment of 'those terrestrial spheres'. The fashion returned to London at the end of the century with the gaslighters, but elegance vanished for their large sheets were illustrated with woodcuts showing the lurid interior of the gasworks. News-agents were another group whose appeal for a Christmas box was a long-established custom, and some of their early sheets are model examples of good jobbing, though the versifiers did not always attain an equal craftsmanship.

During the nineteenth century, postmen and policemen, waits and dustmen joined the soliciting throng, but the fashion began to moderate to a small sheet, unillustrated, and without the lively if sometimes crude originality of its predecessors.

The examination of such appeals suggests that for a short period towards the end of the eighteenth century job printing achieved the elegance so long reserved for engraving. The type designs bought from Caslon and Fry looked well, there was skill in the manipulation of white space, that most difficult art, and standards of presswork were rising. The woodcuts were the stumbling-block. They were, of course, black line, and even after Bewick had revived the craft with his white line, this technique was seldom used in jobbing.

Reynells, who printed the beadles' appeals, advertised their willingness to undertake 'catalogues, handbills, club bills, trades-men's cards and shopbills', a range which showed that little extension of the field had taken place. Nevertheless, Reynells made a success of jobbing and by 1835 had bought a steam press and were using it for the beadles' appeals, the orders for which must have been sizeable.

The low standards exhibited in the jobbing done by Reynells was reflected in other ways. In 1803 the Sunday School Union was founded, an indication of the current interest in religious worship, of which Reynells had already taken advantage in their beadles'

14

Y Was a Youngster that lov'd not
his school,
But trundled his hoop though out of
all rule.

Z Was a Zany that look'd like a
fool,
With his long tassell'd cap he was the
boy's fool.

15

Let all good children come to me,
And I'll learn them their

A B C

A	*A*	J	*J*	S	*S*
B	*B*	K	*K*	T	*T*
C	*C*	L	*L*	U	*U*
D	*D*	M	*M*	V	*V*
E	*E*	N	*N*	W	*W*
F	*F*	O	*O*	X	*X*
G	*G*	P	*P*	Y	*Y*
H	*H*	Q	*Q*	Z	*Z*
I	*I*	R	*R*		

& which stands for and.

Fig. 58. Page size 4 × 3 in.

appeals. The Sunday schools created new work for the job
printer. Tracts and hymn sheets and pictures for the children were
produced in quantity, and Reynells had a sacrilegious idea that
must have netted some profits: they printed a sheet the same size
as the beadles' appeal which purported to recite a letter written by
Jesus Christ. Nor were they content with mere repetition: a note
was added that our Lord would be ready to bestow additional
blessings upon those who bought the sheet and hung it in the
home.

Like the market for periodical publications, the market for job
printers expanded after the Industrial Revolution and cheap
printing was necessarily letterpress. The demand for engraving on
copper diminished, although the engravers kept alive into early
Victorian times the elegance of the eighteenth century. Whereas

the letterpress printers were working on larger and larger sheets, engravers were concentrating on work of a delicacy that the wood-cut could never attain. The circles which were slipped into the backs of watches, giving the maker's name and address, were engraved (see Plate XIV*b*). Working within a diameter of an inch or an inch and three-quarters, the engraver habitually produced not only the name and address set out with elaborate calligraphic flourishes, but illustrations and verses referring to the passage of time. These circles were printed several to a sheet, to be cut up later.

But such skills were more and more rarely exercised. The successful printers were those like Catnach, the ballad printer at Seven Dials, who in many ways recalls John Wolfe. His song sheets, illustrated with a cat, were readily bought by a semi-literate public, who liked the picture and could learn the song. Catnach realized the demand for the ABC—indeed, it was greatly to his interest that the public should learn to read—and his sheets show an improvement on the cramped hornbook alphabet, for they are set out with simple but lively illustrations and large letters.[5]

This new public also influenced the design and content of the lottery handbills. Many of these survive, the result of the large orders given to job printers by the lottery promoters, and they are of high importance in the history of advertising, particularly during the last thirty years when this form of State gambling was legal—the last State lottery was held in October 1826, after which they were abolished.

Hitherto, the most persuasive advertising had come from the salesmen of patent medicines, but there was never in this field the sharp rivalry of a limited number of lottery promoters, engaged in the keenest competition since very high stakes were involved. So, it was the lottery advertisers who are to be credited with infinite invention in matter and in manner presentation, and there is hardly a device of the modern advertising agency that has not been anticipated during the lottery fever of 1800-1826.

Today, for instance, the facsimile letter to the household, to be slipped through the letterbox, is widely used in detergent advertising. But the lottery promoters used the personal letter in 1810 with 'To the Inhabitant of this House' printed from a block of the script made fashionable by the writing-master, Joseph

Carstairs. The composition of the advertising 'copy' showed the same ingenuity. The television advertisers' songs of today have their ancestry in the ballads specially written for 'Bish', the leading firm of the lottery promoters. Other firms introduced themselves with anecdotes or with items of startling information welded to the paragraphs of self-celebration.[6]

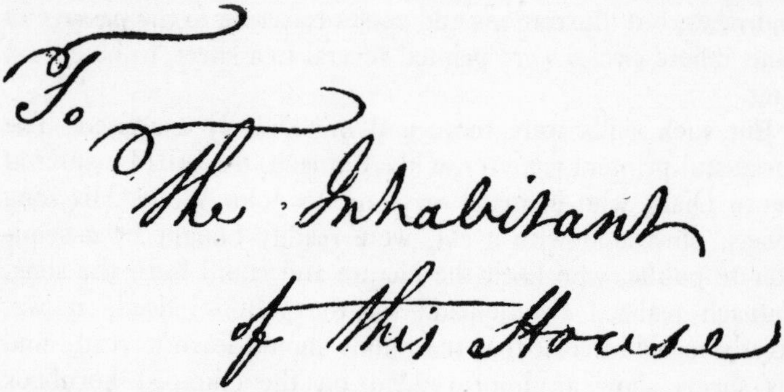

Fig. 59. Width of block 4 in.

Similarly, novelty was sought in the typographical display. The late eighteenth-century bills, like so much jobbing of that period, look attractive still, with their competent use of the elegant display founts cut by Fry, the open old-face titling and Union Pearl. As soon as Fry cut his fat faces, the gross, swollen, deformed letters derived from Bodoni, these founts appeared in the lottery bills. With the same enthusiasm the slab serif or Egyptian face was taken up after its introduction in 1814.

Armed with these two designs, the biggest and blackest letters ever cut in the history of printing, the letterpress job printers found opening to them a new world of display that owed nothing to engraving. No other printers could use these designs, from 6- or 7-line pica, equivalent to 60 or 72 point, to double pica or 24 point. And at last the printers were compelled to use plenty of ink, dense and black, to give the maximum effect of these heavy types and the reverse cuttings which were sometimes made in the large sizes. Sans serif did not become popular as a display face until the 1840s, when it entered upon a supremacy from which it has not yet been ousted.[7]

Whatever we may think of the design of these fat faces and the

slab serif of the early nineteenth century—the R was particularly
ugly—these designs gave a necessary impetus to letterpress
jobbing. As soon as they were available they appeared in any
series that had evolved its form in the eighteenth century—the
appeals of the beadles or newsagents, the lottery handbills—and
the intention was no longer to woo or charm but to batter the
reader into giving his attention. This was a treatment not un-
welcome to the semi-literate classes who were stepping out on
their long road to political consequence.

With the proliferation of display faces throughout the nineteenth century, aesthetic standards in jobbing plumbed depths
never before sounded. There was a compensating factor: the
general standard of presswork rose. The invention first of the
iron press and then of the steam press removed the bottleneck
that had so long existed in the pressroom. It also made possible
greater accuracy in register and greater evenness of impression.
And meanwhile, technical invention proceeded.

Two new techniques became popular. The first was lithography with hand or machine colouring, the latter general by the
1840s. One of the best known and undoubtedly most delightful
uses of this process was for printing the valentine. The early
models were taken from engraving and could not therefore fail to
charm: lithography was cheaper than engraving for the reproduction of the script so essential for the personal message, and the
verses were adorned with the cherubs, draped figures and swags
of flowers that had embellished so much eighteenth-century
work. As hack artists grew more confident in the new medium,
they evolved their own styles, markedly Victorian and remarkably
tasteless. Both St Bride's Institute and Oxford have collections
of valentines, including the cruel contra-valentine, a caricature
and abusive verses sent to a person disliked.

Chromo-lithography was certain to be popular, for never before
had it been possible to print so cheaply and so easily in colour. A
second new technique was often associated with this colour litho,
though it involved letterpress: embossing, sometimes carried to
the actual perforation of the paper. The letterpress printers produced the relief effect by building up the platen to fit a recessed
die, and the process was applied both to their own products and
to those of the lithographers. Valentines were much enhanced by
embossing, as were the envelopes in which love-letters through-

out the year could be enclosed. Sometimes the embossed area was left white, often it was picked out in colour or gold, for wages were low and the cost of an extra working could be quickly recouped.

Envelopes themselves were an invention of the time, the result of the introduction of the penny post in 1840, and the job printers were not slow to exploit the novelty. For sealing, paper wafers were produced, slips smaller than a postage stamp, that could be embossed or printed. If the former, coloured monograms and heraldic devices were suitable in one set of circumstances, but in others a more personal message might be conveyed with an emblem: a pineapple, embossed white on blue or pink, carried the message that 'You are perfect!' but a mushroom indicated 'suspicion'. Some of the most ambitious designs were printed for hotels; the little seal, about three-quarters of an inch by a half, would carry the miniature of the façade as well as the name. When straight text was printed, the message was usually serious and hortatory: temperance advocates would buy blue wafers reading 'the bottle has killed more than the sword'. In such jobbing the smaller and smaller type sizes being cut for newspaper advertising found an ancillary use.

Chromo-lithography and embossing were especially appropriate to jobbing that was to appeal to women. The job printers recognized even more enthusiastically than their contemporaries of the periodical press that there was a market as yet unexploited in this section of the population. The middle years of the century were the golden age of packaging, and particularly of packaging for women; the printer was invoked to embellish any articles likely to be bought in so feminine a manner that they could not be resisted. Hair shampoos, for instance, were sold in packets adorned with an embossed frame, the relief picked out in colour and in gold, and within the frame was an excellent colour reproduction of a sentimental, often pastoral, scene. Colour reproductions were pasted on the lids of handkerchief boxes, the most trivial containers were cheaply and yet exquisitely decorated with colour vignettes.

As never before, there was an attempt to extend the scope of printing, to procure new orders and to encourage, to the profit of printers, new methods of publicity. The inventiveness that had launched Britain on her Industrial Revolution was not lacking in the printing trade. The Collection at Oxford richly demonstrates the range achieved by nineteenth-century jobbing, a range so great that it is impossible to list the many surfaces other than paper that began to carry a printed impression or a transfer. The examples are not only of high technical interest, but rich with ideas for the publicity of manufactured goods.

The outstanding development, however, of the mid-century was the extensive use of colour. It was in miniature for the feminine market or in bold-eye-catching splashes on posters, circus bills or cheap literature in coloured wrappers. Lithography in its early days was more successful as well as cheaper than letter-press, so that by the mid-century there were no fewer than 700 lithographers in London, but standards of colour letterpress rose as the century proceeded and register improved, assisted by the high degree of skill shown by the wood-block makers. [8]

Invitations and certificates offered an enticing field to the job letterpress printer ambitious to use colour and gold. The alle-gorical figures in the classical manner engraved for the plain, monochrome sheet of the late eighteenth to early nineteenth century, were replaced by intricate borders of typographical material, built up with hundreds of pieces and printed in many colours with solid and tint grounds. This was a very different sort of jobbing from that of Catnach and his successors, for it was ordered by the middle-classes, often to be bestowed upon the poor. The numerous societies formed in this reign to promote good works, the growth of Sunday schools, charity schools, mission societies and temperance societies, all the vast exercise of Victorian philanthrophy that was providing at the same time a new market for the periodical publishers paid well for the services of the job printers. And these certificates and invitations and menus, so elaborately designed and printed, admirably conveyed the solid virtues and monumental self-approval of the wealthy middle-classes.

The main impetus to elaborate jobbing superbly executed came from the Great Exhibition of 1851. The catalogue, printed by a firm recently equipped with steam, that of Clowes, was itself a triumphant example of what a job printer could do. The Great Exhibition was followed by the international exhibition of 1862 and the trade's own Caxton anniversary exhibition in 1877. Modern technologists have been tracing their development from that momentous year of 1851. The printing trade owed hardly less to the same inspiration: and jobbing, in particular, was stimulated by the printing ordered before the Exhibition, by the place the trade occupied in the Exhibition itself, and by the orders which afterwards poured in as commerce and industry demanded printed publicity to complete the effect of the Exhibition.

Proximity to the City of London appeared desirable to job printers and there were many small firms in the capital, often dependent upon jobbing alone. They were stocking type as never before, for whereas at the beginning of the century hand-cut letters had provided alternatives to the fat faces, now the new designs required were usually cast. They were buying borders from Germany, such as the Akanthea of Schelter and Giesecke which contained 194 pieces or the Holbein with over a hundred. And in 1877, the year of the Caxton exhibition, a system of specimen exchange was set up, which was regarded as a landmark: 'From the time when Caxton issued the quaint advertisement of the "good cheap" Romish service books used at "Salisbury" down to 1877, when Thomas Hailing of Cheltenham sent out the first number of his famous *Circular*, the progress of job printing in Great Britain had been somewhat tardy, and the innovations denoting advancement artistically, comparatively few.'[9]

Mr Hailing's *Circular* was a clarion call for the specimen exchange, and the bound volumes in St Bride's Library that were the result are an awe-inspiring record of activity in jobbing during the last years of the nineteenth century. But it was not irrelevant to the future of the trade that Mr Hailing lived snugly at Cheltenham. And it was not irrelevant that the past-masters of grandiose jobbing were a Leicester firm, Raithby Lawrence. Their specimens, in spite of the extravagance, assert the vigour and range of the style and amply demonstrate the extremely high standards of presswork that were reached; but this elaborate jobbing was not cheap when London overheads and London wages were considered. City leaseholds and freeholds were rising sharply at the end of the nineteenth century.[10] In 1883 a specimen was acclaimed because it had required 53 workings: the London job printers could find few customers willing to pay their prices. More and more customers found it was easy to order jobbing by post from provincial printers.

During the last decade of the century a reaction against elaborate jobbing must have been welcome to those London firms that remained. It was the influence of the private press movement, and though William Morris himself did not participate in jobbing, leading firms such as the Chiswick Press accepted his teaching and discarded much ornamental material and distorted type designs.

The other inspiration of the time was the *British Printer* which in 1888 came from the firm of Raithby Lawrence with a certain George W. Jones as part-founder. The principles advocated in this periodical, which circulated among and influenced job printers, were: 'graceful type and ornament combinations and dainty printing . . . no very elaborate composition . . . a subtle use of background tints'. A new age began when the adjective 'dainty' was applied to letterpress jobbing.

More potent than Morris in the evolution of this free style was the influence of Ruskin and the Pre-Raphaelites, and the debt was devoutly acknowledged: 'some of the tints', wrote an admirer of the style, 'are difficult to describe, thus fulfilling Ruskin's definition of a true art colour'. Jones reversed the general trend of job printing and came to London, to St Bride Street, Dean Street and Fetter Lane, and in each establishment he not only preached but practised his doctrines.

Jones carried into the twentieth century the worship of presswork and register that he had learnt in the nineteenth. But the type designs of a decade before he would not tolerate. At the turn of the century the Linotype and Monotype hot-metal composing machines were coming to this country from America. The former was not an ideal machine for the job printer, but so high was Jones' standard of craftsmanship that he could accomplish the almost impossible feat of printing a long slug on matt art paper. He was also an excellent salesman, both of himself and his work, one who did not hesitate to combine his doctrines with sound business principles: those with business announcements to make to the public, he declared, must state their case 'in a bold and striking yet chaste and tasteful manner'. Such principles pleased, and so did his colour work and his taste for the rich and sumptuous.

This taste in the hands of the advertising agencies has been the salvation of many job printers, whose heavy bills have been cheerfully met since they counted as 'expenses' when tax claims were made. Without the lavish production of publicity material

N

fashionable since the second world war many job printers would
be unable to meet the necessary cost of new machines and the
rising cost of labour and rent, the latter item one particularly
severe in the neighbourhood of the City. It has not always
been realized that the money so freely spent on printed publicity
material is a form of subsidy that, if cut off, would leave jobbing
in a position not merely precarious but probably untenable.

The needs of the agencies are, in general, adequately met by
provincial printers, and high wages and rents have accelerated
the drift of job printers from the City and its environs. London's
job printing is now a contracted trade and unlikely to revive.
Houses with urgent contracts, such as the Solicitors' Law Stationery Society or Blades, East and Blades, must remain; the Meri-
vale Press is equipped to produce an exceptionally wide range of
jobbing; the Private Printing Office of *The Times* has been ancillary to the main source of revenue. Many of the jobbing houses
were small and few were noteworthy, so that their departure or
disappearance or amalgamation has left little trace, and the
death of Jones in 1942 deprived the London trade of a personality
whose like may not be seen again.

NOTES

1 *Dictionary of National Biography*.

2 This indulgence was only discovered in 1928. It was described in *The Times*, February 7, by Dr A. W. Pollard, and reproduced in *The Library* (1928), ix.

3 Leona Rostenberg, 'Nathaniel Butter and Nicholas Bourne, First "Masters of the Staple",' *The Library* (1957), xii, 23.

4 Sir Ambrose Heal, *London Tradesmen's Cards of the Eighteenth Century* (London, 1925).

5 St Bride's have a large collection of Catnach's work.

6 The British Museum has a number of collections of lottery bills, catalogued under the heading 'Collection'.

7 For a discussion of the origins of slab and sans serif designs see P. M. Handover, 'D'ou vient la lettre que nous appelons l'antique?' in *Monotype Newsletter* no. 116 (Berne, May 1959).

8 According to an appeal preserved at St Bride's there were 700 litho printers in 1854 (St Bride's, Trade Documents, March 4, 1854).

9 George Joyner, *Fine Printing* (London, 1895).

10 *The Site of the Office of 'The Times'* (The Times Publishing Company, privately printed, 1956) gives some account of the rise in freehold prices in the City at the end of the nineteenth century.

VIII

The Decline of Book Printing in London

As job printing in London followed a course separate from that of periodicals, particularly of newspapers, so the course of book printing was equally distinct and had little in common with either. In each branch circumstances and influences differed, typographical needs were not the same, and periods of prosperity did not coincide.

Almost from the beginning of book publishing the interests of the printers had been closely associated with those of the booksellers, their common problem being the protection of copyright. Bynneman, that busy master printer, had been a bookseller with a huge stock of volumes and an owner of copyrights. During the seventeenth century, interests had ceased to be shared. Increasingly, the printers had worked for the booksellers, had even been their 'slaves', so George Wither said. Their habits changed, they ceased to sell books. This divergence must have been uncomfortably apparent during the Commonwealth period, the lean years of the English Stock, when the meagre dividend was swelled by a distribution of Stock books.[1] These were no use to the printers. They had to sell to the booksellers, and it may be imagined what prices they were offered.

The growth of the periodical press was beneficial to the printers: it gave them a chance to snap their fingers at the bookseller-publishers, and to point out that there were better paid printing contracts to be had; though security only came if the printer had substantial shares in the copyright. It was unfortunate that newspaper printing gradually became more specialized, needed certain founts of type, certain sizes of paper and certain modifications to the hand press.

The lifting of the Printing Act at the end of the seventeenth century gave the booksellers considerable disquiet, because it ended the licensing system which had been the foundation of the control of copyright by entry in the register at Stationers' Hall. It was the booksellers who combined to petition Parliament for protective legislation, and it was the booksellers who combined and not the printers or the Stationers' Company as a whole.

In private as well as in public the booksellers were active. One of the principal devices that emphasized their divorce from the printers was the share-book system, of which a specialized aspect was the Conger. This was an organization of any number of booksellers—usually between ten and twenty—who pooled their copyrights and published and sold in collaboration. The aim of a Conger was to protect copyright: if twenty people have a financial interest in a title, it can be defended more effectively against a pirate than by one man on his own.

While they lasted the Congers were powerful organizations: the name was supposed to be taken from the conger eel, that not only deprives smaller fish of food but even swallows them up. A Conger was defined by a contemporary as a set of 'topping booksellers'—perhaps, if a well-known advertising slogan had appeared in 1700 it would have begun 'Topping People take . . .' Each member might put up £100 to buy in likely copyrights, production costs would be shared, and the editions divided between members to dispose of as they liked. An immense number of books went through the hands of the Congers. Fifteen members of one Conger handled over 47,000 books in the year 1704, far more than the Company's English Stock, the mainstay of which was now the almanac and the Singing Psalms.[2]

The Conger system flourished until the mid-eighteenth century and, though short-lived, it and the share-book system of which it was part were means of transition between the old copyright-owning bookseller or printer and the modern publisher who is neither a bookseller nor a printer, though he may have a separate printing works. There was little place for a printer in a Conger, since one of the advantages of membership was that the printed sheets of the editions were allotted to members at cut prices: thus, the price for members of a Conger might be 2s 4d, and the final retail price 5s, with the price to non-member booksellers somewhere between. Very nice; but as the printer now

seldom had facilities for selling books, the cut rate was of no
benefit to him.

One or two printers might be admitted to Congers as a con-
tracting party, but they would be 'topping' printers, such as
Samuel Richardson, well known as a novelist. His was one of the
few important book houses in the mid-eighteenth century.[3]
Baskett, the King's Printer, Woodfall, Bettenham and Bowyer
were the others, to be numbered on the fingers of one hand, and
it is significant that none relied entirely upon orders from the
booksellers. In 1771 William Strahan, by then a 'topping'
printer, referred positively to the slavery in which the booksellers held the printers, and declared that had he confined himself to such printing he might have been able to live, but little
more.[4]

From an analysis of printing costs in the eighteenth century it
appears he was not exaggerating. At this period costing was based
on charges for the single sheet rather than, as nowadays, charges
based on time: when the master printer made up his bill he
added together the charges for composing, correcting and
printing, and to this total added 50 per cent to cover the cost of
the ink, all overheads—such as rent, heat and lighting, wear and
tear on materials—together with his own profits, which, of course,
were the equivalent of his salary as an overseer, for he would act
in this capacity. Paper was the only item that was charged
separately.

The cost for composing a sheet varied according to the size of
type, the area of type on the sheet and the presence of notes.
Correcting was costed at one-sixth of the composing, and the rate
for work on the press was according to a fixed number of sheets,
250 (printed on both sides) being the unit. Thus, a typical cost
sheet might be made up of 8s for straightforward composing in
12 point, 1s 4d for correcting and 2s 4d for the presswork. The
master then added half as much again, 5s 10d, to make the price
charged per sheet to the customer, 17s 6d. If there were 25 sheets
in the book the full bill would be £21 17s 6d of which £7 5s 10d
covered the cost of the ink, the overheads, wear and tear and the
master's reward.[5]

Time was not mentioned. In practice, 250 sheets represented
about two hours' work. An edition of 1,000 copies of a book
containing 25 sheets would occupy one press for three weeks,

working a minimum of ten full hours a day, since the hand press could produce only 125 sheets printed on both sides in an hour. What in fact the master was getting was £2 8s odd per press per week. A master printer with only one press would be lucky if he earned more than his journeymen. Samuel Richardson's rent for the premises that contained his shop and his home was £26 a year. But the master printer's prospects would be brighter with every additional press, provided it was kept fully occupied.

That was the snag. And that was why the chance of periodical printing was eagerly sought by any master printer who had three or more presses—he could hardly have managed it with fewer. The newspaper or magazine would keep the press regularly occupied for a known time on known days. Almost as soon as Richardson began his career he secured a daily and a thrice-weekly printing contract, while he produced only five or seven books a year. At the end of his career he was printing on his own account a *History of the World* that comfortably went through volume after volume, year after year.[3]

We know from Richardson that the booksellers expected to be charged less than private customers, and from William Strahan's ledgers it is clear that they were. When Strahan printed *Tristram Shandy* for Laurence Sterne he charged the author the very high price of £2 10s a sheet. When later he printed the same work for the partners in *Tristram Shandy*, that is, the booksellers, he charged only a guinea. The difference is not accounted for by the changed size—the first was a sixteenmo, the second an octavo, and small type always cost more to compose. The inflated charge to the author was particularly unkind in this case since when Sterne settled an earlier bill he gave drink money to the men in the printing house.[6]

Nor did the booksellers or publishers pay promptly: it is not unusual to find accounts with them unsettled for two or more years. In Strahan's ledger the entry of Bishop Burnet's *Exposition of the Thirty-nine Articles* was typical. Each of the seven partners paid his share individually. The earliest settlement was over a year after the bill was drawn up, and the last, squashed into the margin, seems to have been five years after. The private customer might settle promptly, as Charles Wesley did, when charged £14 for 1,000 copies of a poem to his brother, and he even recalled to Strahan that £1 14s was owing on a previous account, which,

Strahan noted, was 'quite forgot by me, but remembered by them'.[7]

On the other hand there was the poetess, Miss Rodigunda Roberts, who had her poems printed by William Strahan, only 9 sheets, only 500 copies, for which she was charged 16s a sheet early in 1783. William Strahan died in 1785 and not until June 1787 did his heir Andrew hear from her. She then complained that the charges were too high—a complaint with which printers are familiar. He sent a firm note in the third person and the account was settled six months later. As he pointed out to her, the five years for which the money had been owing had eaten away any profit on the job.[8] And whereas the booksellers eventually paid, there were private customers who never did. Strahan's bad debts, which were not many, seem to have been for speeches or tracts printed for noblemen or men in public office.

Strahan printed two periodicals, the *London Chronicle*, which brought in a steady £200 a quarter, and the *Monthly Review*, which produced £80 over the same period. But when he was describing how he had freed himself from slavery to the booksellers, he also attached importance to his share-books, of which in 1771 he had about 200. Then he had his share of the King's Printers' patent and a share of the lawbook patent. His gross income at the beginning of his career was £1,000; by the end it had multiplied tenfold.[9]

Andrew Strahan continued his father's policy except that he disposed of the lawbook patent. His share-books brought him an average of 10 per cent on each investment. The share-book system, more loosely organized than the Congers, continued till the end of the nineteenth century, and even until the second world war there was a survivor in the *Annual Register*. Andrew Strahan's skill and judgment in determining which books to share and how to control the release of editions was much admired by his nephews and heirs, Robert and Andrew Spottiswoode, who continually consulted their uncle on these matters long after he had retired from the business. In 1832 Robert Spottiswoode's half-portion of the family shares was valued at £1,700.[10] But no run-of-the-mill printer could hope to participate in the share-books, and consequently could not hope to obtain the printing contracts derived from them.

Both Samuel Richardson and the Strahans, father and son,

were prominent in the Stationers' Company; but this also was rare for an eighteenth-century printer, although the printers remained loyal to the Company throughout the century, whereas the booksellers did not. Stationers' Hall was still the background against which apprentices were bound and freed. The printers never secured much power in the Company in spite of their numerical strength and at no time did more than seven of them sit in the Court. During the first part of the century the Assistants' places were monopolized by the booksellers, and during the last part by the real stationers, the men engaged in making and selling paper, either wholesale or retail. The rise of this group was due to the demand for paper that followed the expansion of the period-ical press.[11]

The constitution of the Company also changed during this period. During the sixteenth and seventeenth centuries there had been two grades below the Assistants, the livery and the yeo-manry, the latter consisting chiefly of journeymen. During the eighteenth century the liverymen formed two groups and the yeo-manry fell away. By the end of the century the journeymen were combining in trade unions, and in order to negotiate the master printers came together. They held meetings at Stationers' Hall but the discussions upon conditions in the trade took place apart from the Stationers' Company. By the 1830s the master printers were in formal association.[12]

During the eighteenth century the English Stock was yielding a regular 12 per cent yearly dividend, derived chiefly from the Singing Psalms and the almanacs. Though the Psalms ceased to bring in much profit during the last decades, the receipts from almanacs trebled despite any challenge. However, the English Stock no longer had much relevance to the printing trade in London once the printers began to drift away from the Company and to create their own association.

John Walter I was not a master printer and after the trade unions were established he had to employ non-union labour. Like William Strahan, Walter intended to have a finger in as many pies as he could contrive. In 1784 he set up in Blackfriars the Logographic Press, a book-printing house. In conjunction with his book press he also printed a newspaper, and he owned a separate book-selling establishment in Piccadilly. No one could accuse him of being a bad businessman.

Walter had bought an invention for speedier composition by the use of types cemented on one body for prefixes, suffixes and certain syllables. The original purpose of logography, as this use of cemented types was called, had been for the speedier composition of lottery numbers, so that the lists could be completed on the day of drawing. Obviously, increased speed in composition was best demonstrated in a daily newspaper, so John Walter I founded *The Times* (as it was to be known) in 1785; but his book press was much nearer to his heart and for several years *The Times* was no more to him than a piece of advertising for the Logographic Press.

Between 1785 and 1790 a stream of sixteenmos, octavos and quartos poured from the Logographic Press. The letterpress was not, as Walter claimed, 'most elegant'. Bell, who entrusted a manuscript to the Logographic Press, was furious when he saw the result: 'it was not finished with accuracy—on the contrary, it abounded with blunders; nor executed with elegance, for a more slovenly disgraceful performance never came from the office of a printer'. This was somewhat harsh. There had been predecessors of Walter at Printing House Square who would have made a worse job of George Anne Bellamy's Memoirs, but Bell concluded with a crushing reference to 'the incompetency of the Logographic Plan and the confusion of its conductors'.[13]

Walter was not crushed. Stubbornly he continued and in 1789 was claiming that he had at last triumphed over the falsehood and malignity of his opponents, and demonstrated that logography was a national benefit. That was more or less the end of logography. Walter was too busy with his newspaper which, to his surprise, was proving a valuable property. In 1789 he founded the *Evening Mail* as a stable companion and thereafter his compositors and pressmen were much too busy to fuss with the logographic setting of books.

In fact, John Walter I was tackling the wrong problem: increased speed in composing—supposing logography conferred such a benefit—would only accentuate the bottleneck in the pressroom. His son understood the situation more clearly when he sponsored the steam press for more rapid printing.

Apart from his obsession with logography, John Walter I was a typical small printer of the period, with two presses, shrewd enough to see that he would not make a fortune printing books, shrewd enough to make periodical printing pay—he bought a third press in 1794. An even smaller printer who set up at this period was William Clowes I. He began with one press and one man, setting type during the day, printing off in the evening, and distributing the type ready for the following day. During the Napoleonic Wars Clowes secured a contract for some Government printing, and found his salvation in jobbing.[14]

John Walter I was typical of another group of printers when he used the word 'elegant' in connexion with his printing. Although he misapplied the adjective, he was echoing a keen interest in elegant printing that was voiced by a few people in the trade.

Baskerville cannot figure in an account of printing in London, for he belonged to Birmingham, and his name was carefully suppressed by Londoners. The metropolis was not ready to acknowledge any debt to a cross-grained provincial writing-master and businessman who had come late in life to the printing trade. But John Bell of London attended to the revival of good printing in as thorough a manner as Baskerville.

In 1787 Bell was establishing his British Letter Foundry and advertising a forthcoming book as 'the most beautiful book that ever was printed in any country'. The beauty was to derive from his new type design and from the paper and the ink—the last, like the first, prepared by himself. In Baskerville's manner, Bell was making a clean sweep of materials. But he never mentioned Baskerville when he announced that he was determined to rescue English printers from the 'bad esteem' in which they were held, in comparison with foreign artists. Animated by this laudable ambition, Bell flung himself with characteristic energy into the task not only of preparing his new and improved materials, but of publicizing that they were 'new and improved'.

In July 1788, almost a year later, when Bell had issued his first specimen, he addressed the world: 'I have perceived with regret that the Art of Printing has been very much neglected in England, and that it is still in a declining state—expedition being attended to rather than excellence, and temporary gain preferred to lasting advantage and reputation.' Printing, he continued, was 'the happiest invention that ever employed the faculties of man', and 'to retrieve and exalt the neglected Art of Printing in England is the present great object of my ambition'.[15]

Thus, Baskerville was ignored, and Samuel Richardson,

William Strahan and other successful book printers were put in their places. Bell's first publication was to be a Book of Common Prayer, a choice possibly made because Baskerville's ambition had been to print a magnificent Book of Common Prayer. However, the two editions could not be compared, for Bell was not a privileged printer and, audacious as he was, he never managed to produce the protected book. That does not alter the novelty of his statement: that it was to be 'the most perfect and most beautiful book that was ever printed in any country'. In the history of the London printing trade such an ambition had never been voiced.

Moreover, Bell did not limit himself to one fine volume. He applied the principle of periodical publication to his books and issued volume after volume of plays and poems in weekly numbers. The magnitude of his weekly printing orders was increased since he offered several editions: *The British Theatre* came out in three editions, small size on vellum, i.e. wove paper, with engravings, on coarse paper, and on royal paper with extensive margins. He cast widely for customers; there was no question of restricting his fine printing to a limited circle. Each play in the edition of Shakespeare cost only 1s 6d on fine paper and 6d on coarse. The much-vaunted Boydell Shakespeare, on the other hand, cost three guineas for two plays and there was only the one edition, on 'the finest royal Atlas paper'. The Boydell Shakespeare was an entirely different proposition, and in its magnificence it has overshadowed Bell's work and the policy behind his publishing.

The printer was William Bulmer, a Newcastle man who when comparatively young had the good fortune to attract the attention of George Nichol, bookseller to George III, who was then planning with the Boydells an edition of Shakespeare to eclipse all others. Bulmer was set up in a printing house known as the Shakespeare Press, and between 1791 and 1819 this was active under his direction. The first number of the plays established Bulmer's reputation as a fine printer: 'no work of equal magnitude,' it was claimed, was 'ever presented with such complete accuracy and uniform excellence of execution'.[16]

Bulmer was perfectly aware of the ambitions of Baskerville and Bell, for his typefounder, William Martin, was connected with the former, and he himself is supposed actually to have completed his training under Bell. But Bulmer ignored their ambitions and their claims. In his 'Advertisement' to a volume of poems in 1795 he declared: 'to raise the Art of Printing in this country from the neglected state in which it had long been suffered to continue, and to remove the opprobrium which had but justly been attached to the late productions of the English press, much has been done within the last few years'—that is, by the Shakespeare Press. Not only did he suppress the names of those who deserved mention, but the opening sentence of this 'Advertisement' repeats the sentiments, and almost repeats the words, of Bell seven years before. It was a shameless piece of plagiarism.

Bulmer went from strength to strength, and George III is supposed to have become so 'infected with matrix and puncheon mania' that he 'even contemplated the creation of a royal printing office within the walls of his own palace'.[17] No doubt Eyre and Strahan would have thought sourly of that project. Bulmer was a favourite printer of the Roxburghe Club, a blue-blooded association who presented fine editions to each other (and still do). In that Bulmer was employed by publishers (the quondam booksellers) he was a commercial printer like Strahan, but he was undoubtedly pricey, and a list of the books he printed reveals a predominance of de luxe editions of literary classics and folios liberally illustrated with engraved plates. His books were to be looked at by wealthy families rather than read. As a result of this policy, consistently followed, he could retire in easy circumstances after a successful business life.

The verdict of a bibliophile of the time was that Bulmer had brought fine printing into extensive use.[18] But it is questionable that Bulmer did bring it into extensive use. An admirer admitted that this fine printing resulted from new types, excellent ink, and improved printing presses, and, most important, 'a sufficient time allowed to the pressman for extraordinary attention, and an inclination in the employer to pay a considerably advanced price'. Time was a commodity no commercial printer could afford, and Bulmer's achievement was the less in that it depended upon such circumstances. Baskerville and Bell had both seen the importance of type and ink, and Bulmer's claim to an improved press refers only to his patronage of the iron press of Stanhope; he resisted the steam press.

It was pleasant to have been intimate with the royal bookseller and printer to the Roxburghe Club and so to have inspired a monarch that the establishment of a royal printing house was contemplated. But Bulmer made no attempt to face the problems of the printing trade in London. He was overmuch concerned to obliterate the memory of Baskerville and Bell in order to leave himself with the credit of introducing fine printing. He would have deserved more credit if he had demonstrated how the example they set at heavy cost to themselves could be applied throughout the trade. He was not the 'slave' to a bookseller for he was twisting the royal bookseller round his little finger and dictating the 'considerably advanced' prices he was to receive. This was a position very different from that of Richardson or Strahan or Bell—and one far removed from Clowes, with his single press. Bulmer's achievement tended to the creation of a belief that fine printing was a luxury reserved for the rich. 'Bibliomania' was the term, first affectionately but later unenthusiastically applied to a movement that had relatively little influence on, and no relevance to, the London book printing trade.[19]

Thomas Bensley, whose printing house was in Bolt Court, where the London School of Printing now is, was usually coupled with Bulmer as a printer who demonstrated to foreigners that the English Press could 'rival and even excel the finest works' of Continental printers. But Bensley preserved his connexion with the trade. He had a broader experience than Bulmer since he was a partner in the Oxford University Press, and he went about his business of fine printing with less self-consciousness. Most important of all, he supported Friedrich Koenig in the invention of the steam press.

Bensley was one of the three printers who first approached Koenig when it was learnt that he had a trial steam press, the others being George Woodfall, who had a big business in periodicals as well as books, and Richard Taylor, a substantial book printer with a weekly periodical in his house; but Bensley took the lead and was the most deeply engaged financially. However, though a trial sheet of the *Annual Register* (a periodical) was run in 1811, the syndicate made no real progress until John Walter II's interest was roused.[20]

After two machines had been built and were working successfully for *The Times*, Bensley began to experiment on his own, and in 1817 issued a prospectus of a version of the Koenig and Bauer model capable of perfecting, i.e. of printing the second side of the sheet on the one run. There were snags: the cylinders, which were covered with skins, were uneven of surface, and the particular mixture of glue and treacle that clothed the rollers did not give satisfaction. Bensley called in Augustus Applegath, who was later to work for *The Times*. Applegath and his colleague Cowper were faced with a machine that included a hundred wheels: they are supposed to have removed between forty-nine and ninety of them, to leave a perfecting machine occupying half the space of Bensley's model. Even so, the machine was large, with a bed of type at either end and two mammoth impression cylinders—outsize, presumably, in order to allow the ink to dry during its passage from one side of the machine to the other.[21]

Neither Bensley nor Applegath and Cowper derived much profit from their steam perfecting press—indeed, Bensley lost money. But it was remarkable that a London printer should have shown so quick an interest in the greatest development since printing was invented. It is significant that he experimented with a perfecting press: already, the requirements of book and periodical printers were different. The book printers would have liked each section completed as it ran through the press; but, so long as the presses were relatively slow and only one edition was involved, the newspaper printers preferred to work the inside pages later, so that last-minute news could be included.

The four-feeder that Applegath and Cowper built for *The Times* had little relevance to book printing. Presses that demanded more operators were not welcomed, since the flow of work in a book house was not so regular, nor was speed of fundamental importance to book printers. The eight-feeder of 1848 was of even less interest and the rotary Walter Press entirely beyond the experience of the book trade. For much of this period, in any case, these presses were used only in the Office of *The Times*, the only news periodical that had a circulation requiring high printing speeds.

Even in 1819, when the number of master printers in London had almost doubled since 1800, printing houses were still small. Out of twelve described as 'respectable', only three had more than ten pressmen, and six had only four, i.e. two hand presses.[22] In 1826, when Applegath and Cowper were working on the four-feeder, Jacob Unwin could confidently set up in business on his own account in Cornhill with one hand press.[23]

It was possible by means of an inventory to look round Henry Bynneman's premises as they were in 1583 (see p. 29), and it is

possible by means of similar inventories to compare his equipment with that of Andrew Strahan at the beginning of the nineteenth century and of his heirs, the Spottiswoode brothers.

In 1583 Bynneman had cast type valued at £84 and a considerable stock of matrices. In 1800 Strahan had no matrices at all
since he could buy directly from the typefounders; but in both
houses the investment was greater in materials for composing.
Bynneman's three presses had been valued together at £13.
Strahan had nine presses, each worth £13. The difference is
accounted for partly by the rise in prices and partly by the cost of
the metal components in the eighteenth-century press.

Strahan had a stock of cost type far in excess of Bynneman both
in weight and range. The sizes ran from French Canon to pearl,
and his stock of minion, nonpareil and pearl alone was valued at
over £435. He had three composing rooms. Bynneman would not
have more than one, and that was probably shared with the
pressmen: the single pair of tongs and fire-shovel on Bynneman's
premises compare poorly with all the grates, fenders, shovels and
pokers in each of Strahan's composing rooms and in his two pressrooms and warehouse.[24]

Yet the difference is one of scale, and had Strahan possessed
only three presses it is probable that his printing house would not
have been very different from Bynneman's. It is probable that
the 'respectable' master printers of 1819 who had only two or
three presses were equipped in much the same way as Bynneman,
except that they may have held larger stocks of cast type. It was
the additional six presses that enabled Strahan to develop his
printing house.

Between 1800 and 1812, when the next inventory was taken,
Strahan made changes. He had bought a large Stanhope worth
£80 and a small model, £60, besides eight wooden presses designed to give a slightly greater speed. Each of these was valued at
£25. He had made considerable increases in his stock of text types:
469 lbs of a new double pica (2-nick), and over 1,000 lbs of a new
primer, the old being still in use. There was a 2-line pica script—
a new range altogether. The cost had been high, since the price
of metals rose steeply during the Napoleonic Wars. Whereas in
1800 the total value of the printing house was £2,600 odd, in 1812
the type alone was just under £7,000 and the total value was over
£9,000.[25]

Strahan had evidently thought it worth the expense to stock his house with type sufficient to execute the orders for Government printing that were showing a profit of around 216 per cent, and the improved speed of the Stanhopes and the other presses, though slight, was still enough to carry such an expansion. The new material was used for bookwork but, almost certainly, the expansion was undertaken for and financed by the unusual demand for Government printing that attended a state of war. This was the sort of printing Strahan wanted: contracts that were soon worked and off the press, and were paid for at prices he set. Bookwork was secondary; as it always had been in this leading book-printing house.

The bookwork that he did involved editions so often reissued that it became worth while to stereotype, using the plaster-of-paris mould. This process was costly: to compose and stereotype a single sheet might be as much as seven times the cost of composing and printing together. But it saved composing time and released standing type. During the 1820s the amount of stereotyping on Strahan's premises increased so much that a foundry and moulding room were added to the site at New Street (north of Fleet Street). As the larger stocks of type were justified by the demand for Government printing, so the stereotyping was justified by the demand for Bibles; but it was also used for bookwork.

By 1830 when another inventory was made, the Spottiswoode brothers had made relatively little addition to type stocks, although the price of cast type had fallen considerably: 2-line great primer, formerly 1s 3d a lb, to 10d, small pica from 2s 6d to 1s 3d, and so on.[26] In 1835 a list of stereotype editions was drawn up: apart from Bibles, there were twelve octavos, mostly in editions of 500, and many more twelvemos and smaller, i.e. pocket, sizes. The minimum period of reprinting was eighteen months, the maximum five and a half years.[27] The policy of Strahan and of the Spottiswoode brothers was that of the English Stock with the Singing Psalms: to reprint old titles rather than to print new.

Between 1830 and 1832 the Spottiswoodes bought a steam press, an Applegath cylinder perfector, and the pressrooms were reorganized. For the first time there was a division into press and machine rooms. In the latter were the Applegath, valued at £500, and three smaller models at £100 each, besides a Harrild platen machine of £50 and a smaller model of £25. The inventory of the pressrooms reads like a salesman's catalogue: the Spottiswoodes appear to have decided to try one of every make of iron press: a Goulding, a Russell, a Columbian—which was worth £50. Two steam engines were valued at over £550, and the machinery alone was valued at £2,622—roughly, the figure set on the cast type in 1800, only thirty years before. And for the first time an overseer's office was set apart, complete with a mahogany desk.[28]

Thus, within thirty years the cost of equipping an up-to-date printing house had risen sharply, and the printing machinery now accounted for a higher proportion of that cost than in the days of the manual press. After 1832 Eyre and Spottiswoode was a modern book-printing house. The makes of machine might change, the hot-metal composing and casting machines would later be installed and there would be further general expansion, but the problems of high overheads, a longer wages bill and the need for keeping the big presses running would remain. Before 1832 the house was essentially as printing houses had been since the time of Gutenberg; since 1832 the economic problems have not greatly altered.

Few book printers in the first half of the nineteenth century could afford these expensive steam presses. Instead, they bought the numerous makes of iron press that were coming on the market, the Columbian and the Albion from America, the Harrild in this country. Consequently, the book trade was slow to expand.

A perfecting press was sold to William Clowes. He had to buy new premises in order to install the monster, but it proved to be the foundation of his fortunes—indeed, when Applegath and Cowper, unable to dispose of their machines, retreated to Printing House Square, Clowes bought their site by Blackfriars Road. But Clowes did not use the perfector in the first place for books: he printed the *Penny Magazine*, the first periodical to reach a circulation of six figures. It could not have been produced without the perfector; and the perfector could not have been bought or run without such a periodical contract. Jacob Unwin bought a steam press in 1847, and significantly, by 1862, his heirs, the brothers Unwin, were claiming that they printed more than ten periodicals. Clowes and the Unwin brothers, both later principal book houses, repeat the pattern set a century before by Richardson and Strahan, and though they were equipped to print

books they did not rely upon orders from the publishers to keep
their machines in motion.

The invention of new machinery that brought such wealth to
the London periodical printers did not enable the book printers
to build themselves black-glass houses along the City's principal
thoroughfares. The history of the book trade in London ended
early. The book-printing house of Richard Clay at Bungay,
Suffolk, already flourishing in the 1820s, was an example not lost
on contemporaries. In 1867 Watson and Hazell, a firm of periodical printers, set up a branch at Aylesbury, and it was out there
that the book printing flourished: Longman, Macmillan, Rout-
ledge, Chatto and Windus, Hodder and Stoughton, Murray, all
had books printed at Aylesbury.[29] In 1871 Unwin Brothers
secured property at Chilworth, Surrey, and the book side was
worked there, the periodicals only being left in London. And in
1873 the firm of Clowes bought a site in East Anglia which was
gradually developed as the book printing side of their business.

All these firms had felt the same chilly draught from the
competition of Scottish printing. It was the low wages and small
overheads of R. & R. Clark of Edinburgh, Maclehose of Glasgow
and others that forced the book printers to desert London in the
second half of the nineteenth century. Although they had the best
equipment for book printing that the trade had ever known, that
equipment was the most expensive, too expensive for London
rates and wages.

Some remained successfully for a time. Eyre & Spottiswoode
were cushioned by their Bible printing. Cassells at the foot of
Ludgate Hill brought to an unusual pitch the system of publishing in penny and threepenny numbers.[30] The advantage was not
merely that their printing contracts were spread out and the
demand more easily anticipated: they copied the methods of the
periodical press and put advertising on the wrappers. Space was
bought by the manufacturers of soap, blacking and cocoa. This
was a practice more profitable than that of publishers who added
pages of house advertisements at the end of bound books. There is
no hard revenue from house advertisements—as Nathaniel Butter
may have noted when the Commonwealth newspapers began to insert paid advertisements instead of filling space, as he had done, with
a notice of stock at his shop. Cassells subsidized their book printing
by revenue from the advertisements of manufactured goods.

This account of book printing in London has been gloomy. In the sixteenth century the trade was dominated by the monopolists of steady selling titles. By the seventeenth century the printers were said to be in bondage, and in the eighteenth it was thought not possible to make a competent living from mere printing for booksellers and publishers. The invention of new machinery in the nineteenth century made it possible for book printers to survive because they could print periodicals or best-sellers in stereotype editions. If they were not engaged in such printing, they set up their houses in the provinces. Even so, they were more fortunate than the job printers, since they were able in most cases to preserve their identities and to expand.

There is, however, no compelling reason why printing should be performed in London. Print, like soap or cocoa, is manufactured, and it has long been uneconomic to manufacture in the City and its immediate environs. The reasons that force the national dailies to remain do not apply to the rest of the periodical press or to other branches of the trade.

Since the sixteenth century, however, book printing and jobbing have never been a striking economic success in London, and the wisdom of the periodical press when it relied on advertisement revenue is apparent. The book printers of the sixteenth century were wise, too, when they sought to control the trade by restriction and monopoly. It was wise to rely on dividends, on sources of revenues additional to the settlement of bills for book printing. The system broke down in the seventeenth century because the printers yielded to the booksellers too much of their power in the Company and the English Stock, but their decline was halted by the rise of the periodical press in which many of the book printers were active.

Printing is, however, an art as well as a craft, and whether it is in the best interest of that aspect of the trade that printing houses should retreat from the life of the capital is another matter. The successes of the eighteenth century, engraved jobbing, Bell's periodicals and Bulmer's books, were all the result of an intimate relationship between the printer-designer and his customers. The dreadful record of the seventeenth century, when the printers were in 'bondage' to others or dominated by businessmen such as Miles Flesher, John Haviland and Robert Young, is a warning to the printing trade, whether in London or the provinces, that when it abdicates from the responsibility for proper craftsmanship, it cannot be an art.

Though the unions concerned have substantially remained loyal to the notion that printing is a craftsman's job, in their resistance to the introduction of new machinery they have been actuated little by regret that the tradition of craftmanship may be lost, but rather by fear that the journeyman may vanish altogether. And well he may; being too rigidly trained for too long in a craft more strictly a 'closed shop' than, perhaps, any other in this country. The unions have shown no eagerness to adapt their regulations to changing circumstances and they have tended to ignore the experience of the past: that new machinery, by increasing production at lower cost, eventually makes more work for members, not less, and to their profit.

The unionist is, admittedly, in an embarrassing position if he entered the trade with ideals, and it is, perhaps, to offset his embarrassment that he is aggressive. The nineteenth-century compositor wore a top hat and believed himself to be a gentleman, and was incomparably more skilled than his twentieth-century successor sitting at the Linotype—though the latter earns more than many 'gentlemen'. Little has been done by either masters or trade union officials to make him more than a well-paid 'operative'—and the intelligent man resents the fact that 'merit' money is not paid for merit.

Although operatives in the printing unions are so highly paid, they are not among those in the country least determined to strike in order to secure higher wages for less work. The result of this policy is amply demonstrated by the history of the London printing trade. With certain exceptions the trade has successfully shown that it is under no obligation to function in the capital and pay the higher wages there demanded.

The final warning of that history, therefore, is that a time may come when even provincial printers will be unable to compete with the attractive prices offered abroad. Though pockets of printers may survive, as the job printer survives in the City and its environs, there is no guarantee that the story begun in this country in 1476 will not come to an inconclusive end before the close of the twentieth century.

NOTES

1 Cyprian Blagden, 'The Stationers' Company in the Civil War Period', *The Library* (1958), xiii, 1.

2 Cyprian Blagden and Norma Hodgson, *The Notebook of Thomas Bennett and Henry Clements (1686-1719)*, Oxford Bibliographical Society Publications, 1956.

3 William M. Sale, *Samuel Richardson: Master Printer* (Cornell, 1950). This account contains a reference to printing costs and a list of books printed by Richardson.

4 R. Austen-Leigh, *The Story of a Printing House, being a short account of the Strahans and Spottiswoodes* (London, 1912). Strahan's letter is quoted pp. 14-16.

5 I. G. Philip, *William Blackstone and the Reform of the Oxford University Press in the Eighteenth Century* (Oxford Bibliographical Society Publications, 1955), vii. Blackstone's memorandum, pp. 23-38, discusses contemporary printing costs (March 25, 1756) and there is an informative letter to Blackstone from Richardson, pp. 39-44.

6 B. M. Strahan Papers, Add. MSS., 48802. Sterne's own sixteen-mo appeared in 1765, the partners' octavo in 1782. Sterne's earlier bill was for vols. 5 and 6 of *Shandy* in 1761.

7 Strahan's bill for Burnet was dated 1759. See Add. MSS., 48802, which also contains Wesley's bill, 1755.

8 Add. MSS., 48809.

9 Philip Gaskell, 'The Strahan Papers', *The Times Literary Supplement*, October 5, 1956, p. 592.

10 Add. MSS., 489145. The 1832 valuation of the share-books was by Cadell, who was intimately associated with the family's transactions.

11 Cyprian Blagden, 'The Stationers' Company in the Eighteenth Century', *Guildhall Miscellany*, ix (1959).

12 Ellic Howe, *The London Compositor 1785-1900* (London, Bib. Soc., 1947).

13 There is a lively account of Walter's operations at the Logographic Press in *Printing 'The Times' Since 1785* (London, 1953).

14 These and later details about Clowes are taken from the history of the firm, *Family Business 1803-1953* (London, 1953).

15 Stanley Morison, *John Bell* (Cambridge, 1930).

16 There is an account of Bulmer in *William Bulmer and Thomas Bensley: a Study in Transition* by H. V. Marrot (London, 1930). The author urges that Bulmer was a commercial printer. Peter C. G. Isaac, 'William Bulmer, 1757-1830: an Introductory Essay', *The Library*

(1958), 37, gives an excellent account of the main facts about Bulmer. The quotation comes from T. F. Dibdin, *Bibliographical Decameron* (London, 1817, 3 vols.), ii, 384n, a book which was printed by Bulmer.

17 T. F. Dibdin, *op. cit.*, ii, 388.

18 J. Nichols, *Illustrations of the Literary History of the Eighteenth Century* (London, 1858), iv, 697.

19 Dibdin himself wrote *The Bibliomania: or Book Madness* (London, 1809). The changed attitude at the end of the nineteenth century is apparent in John Southward, *Progress in Printing and the Graphic Arts during the Victorian Era* (London, 1897) and the reviews of this useful book (St Bride's, 4004). Whittingham received more credit than Bulmer, but ecstatic praise was reserved for mechanical progress, since this enabled books to be distributed, as they should be, to the bulk of the population.

20 The preliminaries are described in the *History of 'The Times'* (London, 1939-52, 4 vols.), i.

21 These presses are illustrated in Lucien Neipp, *Les Machines à imprimer depuis Gutenberg* (Paris, 1951).

22 Ellic Howe, *op. cit.*

23 These and later details of the firm of Unwin Bros are taken from *A Century of Progress* (London, 1926).

24 Inventory of 1800, Strahan Papers, Add. MSS., 48910.

25 Inventory of 1812, Strahan Papers, Add. MSS., 48912.

26 Inventory of 1830, Add. MSS., 48913. There is a reference to the foundry and moulding room.

27 Stereotype editions, Add. MSS., 48895.

28 Inventory of 1832, Add. MSS., 48914 and 48915.

29 H. J. Keefe, *A Century in Print: the Story of Hazell's 1839-1939* (London, 1939).

30 Simon Nowell-Smith, *The House of Cassell 1848-1958* (London, 1958).

The discrepancy between London wages and those paid elsewhere was brought out in the evidence given to the Select Committee on King's Printers' Patents (1832).

INDEX

BOOKS AND PERIODICALS

INDEX

ornament, 29-31, 63, 68, 82, 99, 103, 114, 139, 140, 144, 181, 192-3, script, 30, 126, 174, 176, 208
Typefounding and founders, 61, 63, 148, 150, 185, 188, 203, 204, 208

Unwin, Jacob, printer, 207, 210-1

Walkley, Thomas, news publisher, 113
Walter, John, I, founder of The Times, 150-1, 201-3
Walter, John, II, 151-4, 157-8, 206
Walter, John, III, 165-6
Walter Press, 166-7, 207
Watkins, Richard, and almanac privilege, 34
Whitchurch, Edward, Bible printer, 76-7
Wicks type-caster, 167

Williams, John, Manager of King's Printing House, 91, 92, 183
Wither, George, author, 51-4, 69
Wolfe, John, printer and news publisher, 38-40, 45, 60-1, 80, 103-9, 110, 113, 148, 153, 155, 169, 174, 187
Wolfe, Reinold, printer, 103
Women, periodicals for, 142-6, 150-1
Woodbine, William, journalist, 161
Woodcuts, 101, 103, 107, 113, 116-7, 135-9, 155, 157, 175-6, 182, 185, 191
Woodfall, George, printer, 198, 206
Wrappers, 141, 161

Young, Robert, printer, 54, 56-8, 60, 85, 92, 212